Neither To Laugh nor To Weep

A gift from **Amaras Art Alliance**

to

Dr. Linda M. Bennett

In appreciation for volunteer optometric services
to humanity in Yerevan, Armenia
Dedicated to the Memory of Antranig and
Santoukhd Malkonian, Troy, NY - Survivors of
the Armenian Genocide in Arabkir, Turkey
Boston, Massachusetts   April 2005

I HAVE DETERMINED NEITHER TO

LAUGH NOR TO WEEP OVER THE

ACTIONS OF MEN, BUT MERELY TO

UNDERSTAND THEM.

—Spinoza

AN ODYSSEY OF FAITH

Neither To Laugh nor To Weep

A MEMOIR OF THE ARMENIAN GENOCIDE

By Abraham H. Hartunian

Translated from the
original Armenian manuscripts
by Vartan Hartunian

New Foreword by Rabbi Earl A. Grollman
Preface by Henry Morgenthau, Sr.
Introduction by Marjorie Housepian Dobkin

THIRD EDITION

Armenian Heritage Press
National Association for Armenian Studies and Research
Belmont, Massachusetts

First Edition 1968
Beacon Press, Boston

Second Printing 1976
Armenian Missionary Association of America
Paramus, NJ

Second Edition 1986, Third Edition 1999
Armenian Heritage Press
National Association for Armenian Studies and Research, Inc.
395 Concord Ave., Belmont, MA 02478

Printed in the United States of America

Library of Congress Cataloging-in-Publication Data

Hartunian, Abraham H., 1872-1939
    Neither to laugh nor to weep: an odyssey of faith; memoir of the
Armenian genocide/by Abraham H. Hartunian; translated from the
original Armenian manuscripts by Vartan Hartunian; new foreword by
Earl A. Grollman; preface by Henry Morgenthau, Sr.; introduction by
Marjorie Housepian Dobkin. — 3rd ed.
        p.   cm.
    Originally published: Boston; Beacon Press, 1968
    ISBN 0-935411-13-5
    1. Armenian massacres, 1915-1923 — Personal narratives.
2. Hartunian, Abraham H., 1872-1939.   I. Title
DS195.5.H33   1999
956.1'00491992'0092
[B] — DC21   97-40141
                                                       CIP
    ISBN-935411-15-1 (pbk.)

BECAUSE my autobiography is tied up with Turkey, the Turks, and Moslems, and a number of European powers, it is natural that I have borne down heavily upon them. But I desire people to know that in my heart there is neither hate nor revenge. I have not written to dishonor anyone. And especially, I have no wish to poison minds against the Turks. I trust that the present Turk is ashamed of what the old Turk did. I trust that the so-called Christian powers of Europe regret the wrongs they heaped upon the Armenians. And I believe that finally, in this world, God's power will prevail, and justice will conquer might.

—ABRAHAM H. HARTUNIAN

TRANSLATOR'S NOTE

IN 1938, my father, feeling that perhaps the story of his life might be of assistance and encouragement to people in what was too often an unjust world, asked me to translate his memoirs into English. Shortly after the task was completed, my father died and the translation remained as the Armenian original—a family treasure.

National and world events since then have indicated to me that my father's account of his life in Armenia should be publicly told.

I was further encouraged in this feeling by my wife Grace and by a fellow clergyman, Rabbi Earl A. Grollman of the Beth El Temple Center in Belmont.

In the publication of the document, I echo the sentiments of my father as expressed in the preceding Author's Note.

Many people have been of help, but in particular I wish to express my appreciation to the Reverend Dr. Dicran Y. Kassouny for his checking of the translation; to Mr. Harold R. Battersby for his transliterations and translations of certain Turkish phrases; and to Mrs. Armine Mardiguian and Miss Susan Haroian for their typing.

—VARTAN HARTUNIAN

June 19, 1968

PUBLISHER'S NOTE
(to the First Edition)

THIS DOCUMENT is the memoir of an Armenian Protestant pastor and community leader who miraculously survived the massacres and deportations of the Armenians in Turkey from 1895 to 1922.

Escaping with his family to the United States, the author wrote this account of the long troubled period. He reveals a human being grappling with evil and malign powers almost too great to be borne or understood; and throughout there emerges the agony and frustration of an entire nation facing obliteration.

The translation was made by the author's son, who was himself a victim of this great tragedy.

In its dedication to the responsible exploration of the human condition through books, Beacon Press finds this document to have peculiar power and reality as well as particular meaning and relevance for the world today.

CONTENTS

Why is a rabbi writing a foreword for a book dealing with the Armenian Genocide? The usual Jewish response to a question is another question: "Why not?"

Perhaps it was *besherdt*, the Yiddish word for "divine providence." Perhaps it was coincidence. But this is how the memoir of an Armenian Protestant pastor came into book form.

Several decades ago, I read a blurb in the newspaper about the fiftieth anniversary of the Armenian Genocide. In truth, I knew little about this event, even though I had been a history major in college. I don't even recall a discussion about this tragedy. At best, this inhuman chapter was but a footnote in the world's chronicles. As a Jew whose destiny was inextricably linked with the Holocaust, I was especially interested in the first genocide of the twentieth century that had taken the lives of one and one-half million Armenians and scattered the remnants throughout the world.

For a briefing I went to visit my dear friend and colleague, the Reverend Vartan Hartunian, pastor of the First Armenian Church in Belmont, Massachusetts. He eloquently described the agonizing episodes in his own personal life and that of his family. Just as I was leaving, he said: "You might wish to look at a memoir of my father that I have translated."

I read it that night. I didn't sleep. I was at his church early the next morning. "Vartan, it must be published," I said. "It will help to sensitize the conscience of the civilized world, not only about your past but the potential for genocide that is still lurking on the dark side of humanity."

I was intrigued to learn that a Jewish United States Ambassador to Turkey, Henry Morgenthau, Sr., had cabled the Secretary of State in Washington on July 16, 1915, that "a campaign of race extermination is in progress under a pretext of reprisal against rebellion." Yet the world was silent.

Was not the Armenian Genocide the harbinger of the Jewish Holocaust during which six million of my brethren were slaughtered? The Holocaust is overwhelming in its scope and shattering in its fury. The death camps were minutely planned and executed over a twelve-year period with the compliance of thousands of German citizens, to the deafening silence of the world. The names of the Jews were carefully chosen, listed, tabulated, and stamped. The Nazis went to incredible lengths to find even a single missing Jew. Unique in all human history, the Holocaust was evil for evil's sake. So was the Armenian Genocide.

Now I understand that Hitler, when he launched his invasion of Poland in 1939, assured his generals that their destructive enterprise, however brutal, would gain the laurels which history reserves for winners. "Who, after all, speaks today of the annihilation of the Armenians?" Hitler is reported to have asked. One demonic precedent ignored by the community of nations set the stage for another.

One day, Reverend Hartunian excitedly called with the good news. A major university press would publish the memoirs. Then months passed. I called him to find out what had happened. He told me that ten Middle Eastern scholars had refused to write an introduction for fear of reprisal from Turkey against possible future research. Even our own State Department urged that it not be published. I thought of the words of Robert Cohen, who wrote in the *Washington Post*: "The process of killing the truth is the last phase of any genocide, and that's what the Turks are doing."

So I contacted my publisher, Beacon Press. This courageous press was the first to publish the Pentagon Papers. The memoirs were enthusiastically accepted. That's how *Neither to Laugh nor To Weep* was born in 1968.

I am writing this foreword because only the truth can set us free. The book of Kohelith, *Ecclesiastes*, provides the following wisdom:

One generation passeth away,
    another generation cometh,
    yet the earth remaineth the same.

I think of these words as I consider the Armenian Genocide and the Jewish Holocaust. The first genocide of the twentieth century took place in 1915. The world was silent. One generation later, the Holocaust took place. The world was silent. Revisionists arose. History was rewritten. Turkish authorities said: "Sure, a few thousand Armenians died of natural causes, but to the contrary, it was the Armenians who massacred the Turks!" And now we read of other historians who claim that for the Jews there was no Holocaust! The crematoria were erected to bake bread for the soldiers. "One generation passeth away."

In 1985, Caspar Weinberger, Secretary of Defense, disdained a resolution to designate a National Day of Remembrance with reference to the Armenian Genocide on the grounds that it would encourage Armenian terrorists. And so the Turks need never acknowledge their guilt.

And need I go into the details of former President Ronald Reagan's tiptoeing through the pages of history? Reagan's reasons for ignoring the Holocaust and the meaning of the Allied victory in World War II were expressed in a press conference in feckless psychobabble:

And I felt that since the German people – and very few alive that remember even the war, and certainly none of them who were adults and participating in any way – and they have a feeling and a guilt feeling that's been imposed upon them, and I just think it's unnecessary.

That statement is remarkable. "A guilt feeling that's been imposed upon them." By what? The Nuremberg trials? Hitler's unhappy childhood? Or by themselves and by the facts of history? And to visit a military cemetery in Bitberg which contains the last resting place for members of Hitler's elite guard, the SS. "One generation passeth away."

I am writing this foreword because non-Armenians, even some of my Jewish co-religionists, consider championing the Armenian Genocide as inconvenient and unwise because of our (America's and Israel's) relationship with Turkey. Remember Ambassador Henry Morgenthau's valiant efforts to save the Armenians during his service in Constantinople. He would have offered his own life, if necessary, on behalf of Christian Armenians. He wrote that as a Jew he could not imagine a nobler cause for which to sacrifice himself.

A Jewish professor of Armenian Studies at Harvard University, James R. Russell, recalls a terrifying picture of a small child in the Warsaw Ghetto with a caption by the Anti-Defamation League: "If the Holocaust never happened, where are the 6,000,000 Jews of Europe?" Dr. Russell appropriately adds: "Where are the millions of Armenians of Sivas, Kayseri, Aintab, Van, Malatia, Urfa, Erzurum?" Whenever one denies reality or camouflages the truth, one should recall the words of Elie Wiesel: "Just as memory preserved the past, so does it ensure the future and our dedication to both."

I am writing this foreword because of the shared experience of Armenians and Jews. We share a history of tears. We must never let the world forget. We must become its conscience. We must never again become silent in the face of persecution and annihilation. As we read this moving book, let us vow not to give Hitler and Talaat a posthumous victory. For we are all survivors. There but for the grace of God we might have been the victims.

While remembering the Armenian and Jewish dead,
And other innocents who were brutally slaughtered,
Let us act for the living.
Let us build upon the foundations of truth.
Grant, O Lord, a life of dignity and understanding
Among all the peoples of the earth,
And inspire us with courage to do what has to be done
To keep alive the memories of the past.

Our task is one . . .
All humankind is one!

Rabbi Earl A. Grollman, DD, DHL
Belmont, Massachusetts

The successful revolution of the Young Turks in 1908, which resulted in the deposition of Sultan Abdul Hamid, was hailed by all the
world as the dawn of a new era for Turkey. Everyone was delighted at
the substitution of a modern, progressive government in place of the
much detested, tyrannous rule of Abdul Hamid. The greatest rejoic-
ings were amongst the Armenians. They promptly offered their assistance to the new Party, which promised equal rights to all citizens
under a constitutional government. I have not the space here to elabo-
rate on the fact that the performance of the Government was a terrible
disappointment after everyone's expectations had been so great. The
massacres at Adana in 1909, and the rapid development of the domi-
neering and chauvinistic attitude of the Young Turks soon dispelled all
the illusions of the Armenians and convinced them that the old rela
tions of conquering and conquered races would continue. The long-
hoped-for equality and liberty failed to materialize. The treatment of
the Armenians became so intolerable in 1913 that they appealed to the
European Governments for relief. After months of negotiation an arrangement was consummated whereby the Sublime Porte permitted
of two European Inspectors who were to have supervisory powers in
the six Armenian vilayets. Messrs. Hoff and Westeneng, the former a
Swede and the latter a Hollander, were appointed. They came to Constantinople for instructions and had not yet been fully installed when
the European War broke out and the Turkish Government promptly
revoked their authority and asked them to leave the country.

The months of August, September, and October 1914, while Turkey was still neutral, proved to be a time which marked great turning-points in the history of Turkey. The Turks promptly mobilized, abrogated the capitulatory rights of the foreign subjects, abolished all foreign post-offices, increased their customs duties, and in every other way took advantage of the fact that the Great Powers were at war with each other. Their success in preventing the Allies from piercing the Dardanelles made them feel like conquerors and awakened in them the hope that they would again become a world power.

The conditions of the War gave to the Turkish Government its longed-for opportunity to lay hold of the Armenians. At the very beginning they sent for some of the Armenian leaders and notified them that, if any Armenians should render the slightest assistance to the Russians when they invaded Turkey, they would not stop to investigate but would punish the entire race for it. During the spring of 1914 they evolved their plan to destroy the Armenian race. They criticized their ancestors for neglecting to destroy or convert the Christian races to Mohammedanism at the time when they first subjugated them. Now, as four of the Great Powers were at war with them and the two others were their allies, they thought the time opportune to make good the oversight of their ancestors in the fifteenth century. They concluded that, once they had carried out their plan, the Great Powers would find themselves before an accomplished fact and that their crime would be condoned, as was done in the case of the massacres of 1895–96, when the Great Powers did not even reprimand the Sultan.

They had drafted the able-bodied Armenians into the army without, however, giving them arms; they used them simply to build roads or do similar menial work. Then, under pretext of searching the houses for arms, they pillaged the belongings of the villagers. They requisitioned for the use of their army all that they could get from the Armenians, without paying for it. They asked them to make exorbitant contributions for the benefit of the National Defense Committee.

The final and worst measure used against the Armenians was the wholesale deportation of the entire population from their homes and their exile to the desert, with all the accompanying horrors on the way. No means were provided for their transportation or nourishment. The victims, who included educated men and women of standing, had to walk on foot, exposed to the attacks of bands of criminals especially organized for that purpose. Homes were literally uprooted; families were separated; men killed, women and girls violated daily on the way or taken to harems. Children were thrown into the rivers or sold to strangers by their mothers to save them from starvation. *The facts contained in the reports received at the Embassy from absolutely trustworthy eye-witnesses surpass the most beastly and diabolical cruelties ever before perpetrated or imagined in the history of the world.* The Turkish authorities had stopped all communication between the provinces and the capital in the naive belief that they could consummate this crime of ages before the outside world could hear of it. But the information filtered through the Consuls, missionaries, foreign travellers, and even Turks. We soon learned that orders had been issued to the governors of the provinces to send into exile the entire Armenian population in their jurisdiction, irrespective of age and sex. The local officers, with a few exceptions, carried out literally those instructions. All the able-bodied men had either been drafted into the army or disarmed. The remaining people, old men, women and children, were subjected to the most cruel and outrageous treatment.

I took occasion, in order that the facts might be accurately recorded, to have careful records kept of the statements which were made to me by eye-witnesses of the massacres. These statements included the reports of refugees of all sorts, of Christian missionaries, and of other witnesses. Taken together, they form an account of certain phases of the great massacre which cannot be questioned and which condemns the brutal assassinators of this race before all the world. Much of the material which I collected has already been published in the excellent volume of documentary material collected by Viscount Bryce.

Henry Morgenthau, Sr.
American Ambassador to Turkey,
1913-1916

From *The Tragedy of Armenia*
(London, 1918)

INTRODUCTION TO THE SECOND EDITION

At first reading, the Reverend Hartunian's memoir is a compelling and moving drama. I myself read it in one sitting, through an afternoon and far into the night. It has all the gripping quality of a manhunt, and indeed during the first fifty years of his life the author on several occasions narrowly escaped death. But beyond the dramatic impact of the story, there emerges from this book a sense of cumulative suffering: of survival through repeated cycles of helplessness, torment, and betrayal. In this sense the book reflects the tragic history of the Armenian people.

Studies of their origin are as yet incomplete, for while certain facts have been established others remain shrouded in myth and speculation. According to legend the Armenians were descended from one of Noah's sons after the landing of the Ark on Mount Ararat. Some specialists believe that the "Arimoi" mentioned by Homer in the *Iliad* may have been among the remote forebears of the Armenians.[1]

It is generally accepted that in the second millenium B.C. Anatolia was settled by people speaking Indo-European languages who migrated eastward from central or south central Europe, mingled with the assorted indigenous peoples of the area—among the most prominent of these were the Urartians, whose kingdom flourished in the first millenium B.C.—and dominated the cultural hierarchy of the re-

---

[1] In recent studies the distinguished Armenian academician Gevorg B. Djahukian has found evidence indicating that the early Armenian language was closely related to proto-Greek.

sulting group to the extent that the Indo-European elements in their language prevailed. Evidence for these facts comes from, among other sources, inscriptions left by King Darius in the early sixth century B.C. which show "Armenia" in the Persian language and "Urartu" in Babylonian, indicating the connection of the two groups by that time. Herodotus, in the fifth century B.C., writes of Armenia in his *Histories*. And, according to Tacitus, by 190 B.C., under their King, Artaxias, the Armenians had united all local groups and achieved cultural unity, with Armenian as the dominant language.

At its height the Armenian kingdom comprised an empire including what is now a large part of northeastern Turkey, the southern U.S.S.R., and northwestern Iran. After 301 A.D., when Gregory the Illuminator converted the Armenian king to Christianity, the Armenian national church—sometimes called "Gregorian" but claiming Apostolic foundations—preserved the cultural identity of the Armenians in the face of successive invasions by Greeks, Romans, Persians, Arabs, Seljuks, Mongols, Tartars, and lastly the Ottoman Turks.

Dominated by the empires of Rome and Persia and, after the thirteenth century, by the Ottomans, the Armenians were at almost every stage of their history beset by tragic alternatives: they could convert and assimilate with the dominant group, or retain their religious and cultural identity at considerable peril.

From the thirteenth to the sixteenth centuries the Ottoman rulers gave cultural and religious autonomy to subject Christians and Jews ("People of the Book") who constituted the farmers, craftsmen, and the chief taxpayers of the Empire. Forbidden to bear arms, these subjects were exempt from military service but had no means of protecting themselves against their Moslem neighbors, and under Moslem law could seek no redress in court. After the sixteenth century, when the Empire began its long decline, corruption seeped down the ranks from the Sultans' viziers to the lowliest governmental officials in the provinces. Bribery and illegal taxes proliferated, and the central government moved increasingly unruly Moslem tribes (who by now constituted a vast, unemployed army) into the predominantly Armenian provinces where they could harass, pillage, rape, and kidnap the unarmed Christians with impunity. The result was the dispersion of Armenians throughout the Empire and, for the more fortunate, to other nations. But the condition of those left behind became correspondingly more precarious.

At its height the Ottoman Empire stretched to the gates of Vienna in the West and North Africa and the Persian Gulf in the South and East. But after the Greeks fought for and gained their independence (with the assistance of England and France) in the early nineteenth century and other restive European subjects in the Balkans rebelled and followed suit, Eastern Anatolia (where the Armenians were concentrated), without commercial resources, held little interest for the European Powers.

By 1914 approximately 1,700,000 Armenians lived in the Russian Caucasus and controlled much of the wealth of Tiflis and Baku. Others had become established in the great cities of the West as well as in India and the Far East. From their safe havens, diaspora Armenians often exhorted their Turkish-Armenian kinsmen to rebellion, with no success. Armenian groups did form political parties in the last decades of the nineteenth century, but their primary aim was the establishment of reforms in the Ottoman Constitution and a measure of autonomy and safety in the northeastern provinces, where intolerable conditions and periodic massacre had become endemic. But England, while bemoaning the treatment of the Armenians, was virtually in control of the dissolute Empire and discouraged political reforms which might have lessened that control. And wealthy European merchants, established for generations in Constantinople and Smyrna, were exempt from all taxes and held diplomatic immunity from Ottoman law. They found the *status quo* ideal, for it was the very lack of reforms in the Empire's treatment of its Christian subjects that provided the justification for exceptional privileges (called "capitulations") given to foreign residents.

The Crimean War (1851-56) and the Russo-Turkish War (1877-78) had resulted from Russia's endeavors to penetrate Turkey by acting as protector of the Armenians, whose plight was merely worsened when England and France refused to allow Russia that privilege. Indeed, the Armenians had enormous problems in Turkey, but the so-called "Armenian problem" (alternately referred to as "the Armenian Question") was both created and exacerbated by the European Powers.

Economically defunct and in need of a scapegoat, the Turkish gov-

xix

ernment would turn on the Armenians. Among the Powers there would be a great deal of talk and shaking of heads on all sides; the talk would enrage, and the lack of action would encourage further massacre. By the end of the nineteenth century nearly half a million Turkish-Armenians had been slaughtered, 300,000 of them in 1895-96 by order of Abdul Hamid II, aptly called "the bloody Sultan."

Beginning in 1820, hundreds of Protestant missionaries were meanwhile arriving in Turkey from America. They set up and staffed schools on the American model—by 1915 there were well over 500. The Armenians welcomed what they perceived as foreign interest and therefore protection. They were moreover excited by the Western education brought by the missionaries, and made up a large proportion of the students in these schools. The explosion of American-style religion as well as educational opportunities into the remotest areas of Turkey also encouraged some Armenians, such as the Reverend Hartunian, to espouse the more Evangelical Christianity of the missionaries. During the First World War and until the United States entered against Germany and diplomatic relations with Turkey were broken, many missionaries stayed in Turkey and were eyewitness to the Genocide of the Armenians in 1915-16, as their predecessors had been to the earlier massacres.

The outbreak of the Russian Revolution proved yet another disaster for the Armenians. In 1917 Russia made a separate peace at Brest-Litovsk and returned to Turkey the bordering provinces to which tens of thousands of Armenians had fled over the frontier during the Genocide. Under the terms of the treaty which was concluded, the Armenians were allowed a small, independent state. They had already set one up after the area was abandoned by the Russians, and it had almost immediately been invaded by the Turks, who now, the Treaty of Brest-Litovsk notwithstanding, attacked with even greater ferocity while the Armenians fought back with equal ferocity.[2]

The armistice in 1918 brought no relief to the Armenians; the Allied leaders meeting in Paris had other priorities, namely a settlement with Germany. In 1920, under the Treaty of Sevres, they were promised a

---

[2] It was during this time that Armenians in this region killed Turks, including innocent civilian Turks, and not, as Turkish historians now claim, during the Genocide of 1915-16.

much larger state with boundaries drawn up by President Wilson himself, who counted on an American mandate over the area. But the Sevres treaty, never ratified by any of the Allied Powers, was outdated even before its terms were revealed. Political realities had swiftly overtaken the promises made to the Armenians and others in wartime, and none of the provisions of the treaty were ever adhered to. The net result of the treaty was simply to outrage the Turks into rallying behind the insurgent leadership of Mustapha Kemal (Ataturk). In truth, after 1919, the Allies had swiftly reversed their earlier edicts and begun courting Kemal's emergent leadership, each behind the others' backs. Their chief aim: to gain the exploitation rights and attendant commercial advantages to the oil of the Mosul, until then the greatest oil find in history. (It belonged to Turkey until 1927—thereafter it became Iraq.) The new technology was proving its thirst for this commodity; as Henry Berenger wrote to French Premier Clemenceau on December 12, 1919: "He who owns the oil will rule the world." The Armenian lands held no such precious resource, and as Admiral Mark Bristol wrote to a fellow admiral from his post as American High Commissioner in Constantinople, "We would be taking the lemon" [in accepting a Mandate over Armenia].[3] After the proposal for a Mandate was defeated by the United States Senate, the only choice remaining to the starving and beleaguered Armenians in the Caucasus was to have their sole remaining province of Yerevan fall into Turkish hands or to cede it to an approaching Soviet army. Under the circumstances it is not surprising that they chose the latter. In the Armenian SSR (the smallest of the Soviet republics) over three million Armenians now live with a surprising degree of religious and cultural autonomy, while the few Armenians remaining in Turkey are finding it increasingly expedient to assimilate.[4]

Readers of the Reverend Hartunian's memoirs will note the extent to which he relates the story of the treatment of the Armenians in Turkey between 1895 and 1922. Having lived through no less than seven separate massacres, including the Genocide of 1915 and the coda—the burning of Smyrna in 1922—the Reverend Hartunian embodies the

[3]Letter, Admiral Bristol to Admiral W.S. Benson, June 3, 1919, Bristol Papers, Library of Congress.

[4]The best available estimate places the number of Armenians living in Turkey at the present time at 65,000. See the survey by Armenag Voskanian in *Lraper*, social sciences monthly published by the Academy of Sciences of Armenia, September, 1985.

Armenian experience of those years. Although a case history does not in itself constitute historical proof, each segment of his adventures has been corroborated by hundreds of other escapees and by eyewitnesses (chiefly American and German) whose testimonies are on record. Evidence rests in the archives of the United States, Great Britain, France, Italy, Greece, the U.S.S.R., Bulgaria, and Germany, among others. (And it is worth emphasizing that Turkey was Germany's ally during World War I.) The very fact that this is a true story is vitally important to bear in mind in a day when the present Turkish government is orchestrating—at great expense and effort—a denial of this history so frenetic as to make even the uninformed question why this folk "doth protest too much."

No amount of money and propaganda disguised as scholarship will succeed in changing the historical record. Still, books such as this are essential because the public perception must reflect historical facts. Balanced as we are on the precipice of omnicide, the terror of our predicament lies in our inability to distinguish good from evil and in the very real possibility that the next cataclysm will result from evil disguised, or even intended, as good. At no time in history has it been more important for recent generations to understand clearly the nature, the causes and effects, of earlier horrors and to avoid the dangers of indifference, of deception, and worse, of self-deception. It is to be hoped that the Reverend Hartunian's story will lead to further study and reflection.

There is no ambiguity in his story, yet it is in great part owing to the narrator's pervading wisdom that we cannot (and most certainly must not) forget that the human capacity to commit "crimes against humanity" lies within man's nature. So it is on this level of the book that its deepest value lies, for it raises the most fundamental questions about the nature of man and God. Beyond the question of why evil exists, of why man perversely enjoys inflicting suffering on the innocent, of why God allows this, is the question of how innocence and faith can be sustained in the face of unremitting pain. The book also raises the issues of forgiveness and justice. A true Christian, Abraham Hartunian tells us that he carries in his heart "neither hate nor revenge," that he trusts "the present day Turk is ashamed of what the old Turk did…," and that he believes, eventually, "justice will conquer might."

When he speaks of justice, as a man of the cloth, it is surely not of human justice, so often indistinguishable from revenge, but rather Divine justice which is not ours to dispense, which is a part of Divine Grace, and which must be preceded by repentance.

Yet surely a measure of Divine justice is in evidence when one considers that the remnants of the Armenians, decimated and scattered to the winds, have adapted to new homelands, multiplied, and prospered, while continuing to maintain their identity. Today, there are more than double the number of Armenians in the world than were living when Ottoman policy sought their extinction. This in itself is something of a miracle, and it goes far towards vindicating the Reverend Hartunian's faith.

Marjorie Housepian Dobkin
Barnard College
Columbia University

April, 1986

After this incident, one day, as I was conversing with a Turkish official, he said to me, "My friend, there is no hope. No longer can the Turk and the Armenian live together. Whenever you find the opportunity, you will annihilate us; and whenever we find the opportunity, we will annihilate you. Now the opportunity is ours and we will do everything to harm you. The wise course for you will be, when the time comes, to leave this country and never to return."

This Turk had spoken the truth. No longer could the Turk be a friend to the Armenian, or the Armenian a friend to the Turk.

PART ONE

1872–1914

1

My BIRTHPLACE was the city of Severek, in the vilayet of Diyarbekir, one of the eastern provinces of Turkey and at one time part of the land of Armenia. The date of my birth was August 10, 1872. My father's name was Harootune; my mother's, Heghineh; our family name was Dabbaghian. *Dabbaghian* means "tanner of hides" in the Turkish language. When I came of age and committed myself to Christ as my personal Lord and Savior, I changed my name to reflect my new status, like Saul who became Paul. *Harootunian* (Hartunian) means in the Armenian language "one who has been resurrected from the dead."

My father had had no schooling, but he could read and write and was very fond of the Bible, which he studied continuously. He knew the value of education and used to encourage it everywhere. From the very beginning he was a firm believer in the Armenian Evangelical Movement and a member of the Armenian Evangelical Church. A church-lover and devout man, he kept his family circle in a religious and spiritual atmosphere.

My mother was educated. She had received the best instruction of her time and had served her nation for many years as a teacher. She was a refined, God-fearing, kind woman, like her namesake, St. Heghineh.

My father was married three times. He had two boys and two

3

girls by his first wife, a girl and two boys by my mother, but no children by his third wife. Since my sister and brother died in infancy, I was my mother's only child, and much beloved.

My father was not rich, but by his industriousness as a tanner and shoemaker he was able to provide the daily household necessities and to maintain the comfort of the family.

I was indeed fortunate to have had devout parents. My mother dedicated me to God even before I was born. She brought me up with her prayers and pious songs. The major concern of my parents was to be attentive to my moral and spiritual condition, so that when I began to know myself, I found myself in a sanctified environment. My first six years were spent around the sacred family table, swept by sweet-scented incense, in Sunday Schools, sometimes kneeling with my parents before the church altar, learning short prayers and songs and verses from the Bible. And in this way my soul and mind received nourishment by accepting the tiny drops of heavenly manna. Blessed days!

But, alas, only six years, and my dear mother was snatched away from me and I was left an orphan. My mother had a most tragic death, the recollection of which appals me even now.

My mother had rheumatism in her legs, and she was greatly troubled thereby. She had applied many remedies but had found no relief. One day, from the village of Chermoug, about forty miles from Severek, an Armenian woman came to the city announcing herself a specialist in rheumatic ailments. My grandmother, my stepsisters, my aunt, and some women of the neighborhood gathered together, considered the matter, accepted the suggestion of this *ebbe* (midwife), and decided to try her. Without telling my father, they proceeded. A large caldron was brought and filled with hot water. My mother was told to prepare herself. I remember that, according to her custom, she took her Bible, read it, closed her eyes and prayed. Then, moving slowly from her place, she approached the caldron and climbed into it. The water was very hot. "I can't stand it!" she cried out. A little cold water was added, but still she cried out, "I am burning!" The *ebbe* ordered the women not to heed these cries, so they forced my mother to sit down in the hot water. Rugs and quilts were thrown over the caldron so that the steam might be

4

shut in and, by a thorough perspiration, the patient might be healed. My mother had gone mad under the covers and was screaming. But the *ebbe* was not moved. My mother began to tear the quilts with her teeth. This too was prevented. Finally her struggle ceased. Silence prevailed. The *ebbe* said happily to the women around her, "See, she is resting. She no longer cries out. She is healed." The set interval passed. The covers were removed. In truth my mother was resting. My mother was dead.

At this time my stepsisters were already married and there was no one in the house to take care of me. My father and stepbrothers, Hagop and Yeghiazar, were busy with their trade. My father entered me in kindergarten.

In the mornings he got me ready, gave me breakfast, prepared my lunch, and sent me to school with my satchel slung over my shoulders. Then, locking the doors of the house, with my stepbrothers he went to his work. After school was over, I went straight to his shop and we all returned home. My stepbrothers prepared supper and, the meal over and the dishes washed, we spread the beds on the floor and slept.

Three years passed and my father married a Syrian girl by the name of Sara. Now the doors of our house were again unlocked during the day. This woman loved me as her own child and I began to have a happier life.

By the time I was fourteen I had completed the course at the local Armenian school. These eight school years prepared me well for my future work. My mind was enlightened. My moral life and character were set on firm foundations. Spiritually I was more conscious and reflective. My piety had lost its primitive and inherited nature and had become a fact of personal experience. Sunday Schools, Christian Associations, prayer meetings, church services—these were my dearest pleasures.

I had a firm belief in divine providence and protection. Knowing God as my Father, I was happy beneath his watchfulness and care. I loved his work and had a strong desire deep in my heart to extend it to a wider field. My childhood dream was to see myself one day high in a pulpit, imparting the message of God to the people.

Life was not always pleasant. One day, while at a Turkish

bath, I was playing with my friends on a high ledge. I slipped and fell to the stone floor below, knocking myself unconscious. A number of times the Armenian children of the neighborhood stoned me and wounded my head and face. Once my eyes became infected and I suffered severe pain for months. All hope was lost for my sight. But time saved me from blindness.

When my childhood years ended, I longed to attend the American college in Aintab, but my father was not able to send me. My appeal to the college administration, asking assistance, was fruitless and I was rejected. The day came when my father, holding a shoemaker's apron in his hand, said to me lovingly and sadly, "My son, it seems that for the present I shall have to take you to the shop to work with us, until the Lord prepares the way for you to attend college." He slipped the apron over my head and kissed me. My eyes filled with tears but my heart obeyed, and I joined him and went to the shop and began to work. Five long years passed in this way. I had no success in mastering the trade.

However, I attended all religious services, studied my Bible, and prayed. And in order not to forget what I had learned in preparatory school, I went over my studies again and again, never letting go the hope that one day the propitious moment would come when I should continue my education.

During these years my two stepbrothers were married and we were blessed by two cherubim—the ornaments and darlings of the house. We were a happy family of nine.

But one day I too, like my mother, suffered a terrible rheumatic attack. I was paralyzed for months. At another time I came down with typhoid fever, and cold death sat ready near my bed. My elder stepbrother's young wife and two children died one after the other, and the family was afflicted with lamentation and grief.

The summer of 1891 brought the realization of my dreams! I was sitting in the shop behind a shoemaker's block, busy with my daily task, when I had a visit from Hagop Najarian, the son of the pastor of our church, Rev. Vartan Najarian, later pastor of the Third Armenian Evangelical Church of Aintab, and martyred in 1915 in the deportation massacres. "*Achkud*

6

looys. Congratulations!" he said. "My father has received a letter from the college, saying you have been accepted and your tuition will be paid! You must leave in a few days."

What happy words! Together with my father we hurried to the pastor to learn the details. That very day I began to prepare for the journey.

My stepbrothers were reluctant to have me go, objecting that I could be useful to them in their work. But that dear father of mine would not let this opportunity slip. I know he had no money. Without the knowledge of my stepbrothers he borrowed money at interest to take care of my needs and put me on my way with his prayers, blessings, admonitions, and kisses.

Saying farewell to my birthplace, my family nest, my loved ones, my church, my beloved father, and to the sad grave of my sweet, angelic mother, in tears and in smiles, I set out, and arrived a few days later at Central Turkey College in Aintab.

It was September of 1891. In the beginning of this year the college building had caught fire and two-thirds of it had burned. Although rebuilding had been undertaken immediately, the work was not yet completed, so the opening of the school was postponed. Like many others, I made use of this time to earn a little money by working as a laborer.

My father's good habit remained with me as an inheritance, and I decided from the first day to appropriate regularly a tithe of my earnings for religious and benevolent purposes. My first two *metelikler*, about two cents, which I earned by carrying water to the president's house, I gave on the following Sunday as an offering to the poor.

Early in October the school year began. Failing in my examinations, I was registered as a junior in high school. I continued my studies uninterruptedly for four years, however, and successfully completed my sophomore year of college.

When I first came to college I was the object of laughter and scorn of the students, and even of the professors. My clothes were poor, my ways clumsy. Wretched and helpless, I wept continually. The remembrance of former days brought a deep longing for them. My only sources of consolation were my Bible, my meditations on spiritual things, and my prayers. But as the years passed, I found my way into the esteem of both my professors and my peers. In the spring of 1892 I applied for church membership to Rev. Kara Krikor, pastor of the Second Armenian Evangelical Church of Aintab, and was accepted. I was a member and several times president of the college Y.M.C.A. I taught in churches and Sunday Schools. I organized prayer meetings in different sections of the city and conducted a weekly religious service for the sick in the American hospital. In order to meet my school expenses I was obliged to work, and especially during the summer vacations I worked hard, waiting on the tables of the students, cleaning schoolrooms and preparing lanterns, watering the gardens of the missionaries, chopping wood for furnaces, carrying stones and soil on my back.

Because of my older age, my friends called me "Father"; I became known by this name in the college and throughout the city. Evil habits, it seemed, flourished among the students. But that character which had been formed in my family circle for nineteen years kept me firm and I was uninfected. Indeed, rather than being influenced myself, I was able to lead others toward the good. Not, however, without enduring some ridicule. One night when all the students were asleep, I knelt on my cot and prayed silently, according to my custom. I prayed long and then went to sleep. Suddenly I awoke, aware that I was being borne aloft. Low voices were singing: "Toward heaven, fly toward heaven. Fly to God." My dormitory mates were carrying my cot in the air. When they saw I was awake, they left me in the middle of the room and scurried to their places.

The college had set aside Saturday mornings for composition and oratory. Although not successful in composition, in oratory I always received a high grade, and in my sophomore year, in the presence of a large audience, I was awarded the prize for the best work in this field.

In the spring of 1892, my first school year not yet ended, I suffered severe pain in my eyes. Gradually it increased till it was unbearable. Finally I went to the city and had my eyes examined by the able and well-known Dr. Shepard at the American hospital. He turned to me after the examination and said abruptly,

"There is no hope at all for your eyes. You cannot study longer. You must leave school at once."

I was horror-stricken. My eyes filled with tears. I said trembling, "But Doctor, you know my desire is to finish college and then theological school and to become a minister of the Gospel. Are my hopes vain?"

This time compassionately, he answered, "It seems that Providence does not consider that work proper for you."

I returned under a heavy burden. Badly in need of rest and comfort I withdrew to my room and presented the matter to my Heavenly Father. And a voice spoke to me: "Fear not, my Son. I will help you. I will preserve your eyes. I will accomplish your desire." When I arose, I was well. Not Dr. Shepard's word, but my Heavenly Father's, prevailed. Visually uninterrupted, I completed college and theological seminary, for twenty-three years carried on my religious work, and was accepted into America. The same eyes serve me now as did forty-six years ago.

2

In June, 1895, with the college closed for the summer and my sophomore year completed, I received an invitation from the First Armenian Evangelical Church of Aintab to teach in its schools for a year. I personally was anxious to do the work, and several of my professors encouraged me in this direction.

At the same time, however, a similar invitation reached me from Severek. The president of the college, Dr. Fuller, and a traveling missionary, Mr. Sanders, thought it proper for me to accept the latter invitation. Convinced that my first duty was to my native city, I agreed and returned to my birthplace.

My stepbrothers now had their own homes. I stayed at the house of my father and stepmother. I was happy to be here again, in my church, surrounded by my friends and loved ones. The summer months passed pleasantly.

On Monday, September 16, the school was opened. From the very first day, Protestant and Armenian Gregorian children crowded the rooms. The students were classified and books were distributed, and the first hopeful step forward was taken.

We enjoyed an unforgettable seven weeks. The moral and spiritual atmosphere of the school was enviable. My pupils and I were tied together with the bonds of love. But suddenly the dark and horrid week beginning Sunday, October 27, was upon us. The rumors of terrible massacres and plunders spread everywhere. The whole Armenian community as one body felt its impending doom. Each hour of that week passed in fear and trembling. Even in this consternation we continued our schoolwork through Friday, November 1. In the afternoon I knelt with my dear children and prayed. Then I shook their hands, committing each one to the mercy and protection of God, and sent them home.

In the city of Severek there were more than thirty thousand Moslems, and the surrounding villages, over four hundred of them, were crammed with bloodthirsty and savage Moslems— Turks, Kurds, Arabs, Circassians, Chechens, Zazas. The Armenians were a tiny minority—about seven thousand unarmed, unprotected, innocent people. Those great mobs both inside and outside the city were armed with all kinds of deadly instruments and were waiting impatiently for the order to massacre.

It was Saturday, November 2, 1895. The Armenian men, according to their custom, had gone to their shops and were busy at their trades. The women and children were in their houses or, worse, in the public Turkish baths. All at once the city was surging with mobs, tumultuously alive with human wildness and desolation. The butchers were eagerly sharpening their knives and axes, and those to be slaughtered, wringing their hands, were groveling and bewailing the inevitable. On Saturday afternoon I was at home with my stepmother when the women and children of the neighborhood began crowding into our yard, weeping and anointing their heads with dirt because their Turkish neighbors had told them the massacre was about to begin. I hurried to the bazaar and soon reached our shop, where I sat down, unable to speak. In silence I took my last farewell from my father and tearfully returned home. The final hour had come. I had not one word of comfort for those wretched women waiting for me.

Hardly half an hour passed and I had an impulse to go to the bazaar again. I do not know why. As I leaped out into the street, I saw a young man whom I knew, Kevork Sevdalian, running hatless, breathless, toward his house.

"What's the matter?" I asked.

"Go back!" he shouted. "They've started!"

Where should I go? To the church! To the pastor! I ran in that direction.

Turning a corner, I suddenly beheld a wild mob about to attack the Gregorian church. When they espied me, they shouted, "*İşte bir kâfir! Acele eddin ve onu geberddin!* An infidel! Hurry and slay him like a dog!"

I turned back, and, finding the street door of an Armenian house open, I ran in, climbed the stairs to the roof, hurried over several more roofs, and, jumping down on a wall, found myself in the yard of the Protestant church. There was my beloved pastor, Rev. Mardiros Bozyakalian, cane in hand, walking to and fro.

"What are we going to do, Pastor?" I asked.

"Nothing, my son," he answered, "but pray and wait."

Now the whole city was baking, burning, boiling. The barking of guns, the clashing of axes, the tumult and shouting of the mobs of the streets, the plunder, the moaning of the wretched and unprotected, and here and there the flames and crackling of the houses of Christians had transformed the city into a hell. The butchers had lost all conscience and pity and were searching for victims to attack, for women and young girls to rape, for property and merchandise to plunder.

I followed the pastor to the other side of the yard into the school building. On the second floor, where I had enjoyed those seven weeks with my pupils, we found thirty-seven others— women and children and a number of young people, among them the pastor's wife and sons and daughters. They had come from neighboring houses to find refuge there; all, weeping and sobbing, awaited an agonizing death.

Convinced that the hour of farewell to life was about to strike, and knowing that I was in Gethsemane and had need of help from above, I went alone into another room and presented myself to my Heavenly Father. I poured out my condition to him, besought his help, assured him that I wanted his will to be done, and pleaded that, if it were possible, he save me, but if not, he prepare me for martyrdom. And my Father heard. He sent down his angel from above—that same angel who brought strength to One about to die in Gethsemane—and strengthened me. I had a new peace, a new calm. I saw God the Father and his only Son, Jesus, standing at his right hand.

Returning to my friends I tried to comfort and encourage them. I asked our pastor to pray, that we, kneeling, might partake in the prayer. But the pastor was profoundly disturbed and could not pray. Therefore I myself knelt down and spoke to God, and the rest took part with their amens.

All this lasted about half an hour. The mob had plundered the Gregorian church, desecrated it, murdered all who had sought shelter there, and, as a sacrifice, beheaded the sexton on the stone threshold. Now it filled our yard. The blows of an ax crashed in the church doors. The attackers rushed in, tore the Bibles and hymnbooks to pieces, broke and shattered whatever they could, blasphemed the cross and, as a sign of victory, chanted the Mohammedan prayer:

> *La ilaha ill-Allah*
> *Muhammedin Rasula-llah.*
>
> There is no other God but one God
> And Mohammed is his prophet.

We could see and hear all these things from the room in which we huddled.

From the church they headed toward our building. They were coming up the stairs. A few of the stronger women in the room closed the door and stood against it, thinking in this way to prevent the entrance of the enemy. But before savage force they gave way, and now butchers and victims were face to face.

The leader of the mob cried, *"Muhammed'e salâvat!* Believe in Mohammed and deny your religion!"

No one answered.

I approached him and said, "Effendi, you see that they are all women and children. Have mercy on them and spare them. If you want booty you can take whatever we have. Have pity on us."

Squinting horribly, he repeated his words in a terrifying voice: *"Muhammed'e salâvat!"*

Not one of us was willing to deny his beloved Savior and to betray Christianity to save his own life.

The leader repeated again: "*Muhammed'e salâvat!*" and gave the order to massacre.

The first attack was on our pastor. The blow of an ax decapitated him. His blood, spurting in all directions, spattered the walls and ceiling with red. Then I was in the midst of the butchers. One of them drew his dagger and stabbed my left arm, and I, convinced that they were about to torture me, instead of remaining standing, squatted on the floor with my head bent in front of me. Another second, and I lost consciousness. I felt as if I were in a dream and were flying down from a high place, and I remember clearly saying in my mind, "I shall see God. I shall see God."

What happened to me some women who had remained alive told me later. When I squatted on the floor, three blows fell on my head. My blood began to flow like a fountain, and I rolled over like a slaughtered lamb. The attackers, sure that I was dead and seeing no need to bother further, left me in that condition. Then they slaughtered the other men in the room, took the prettier women with them for rape, and left the other women and children there, conforming to the command that in this massacre only men were to be exterminated.

Blood-drenched and unconscious, I remained stretched out on the floor, surrounded by mutilated corpses, for seven hours. Sometime after midnight someone shook my body and consciousness returned. A blustering wind was blowing through the open windows and door of the room. It was bitter cold.

There is someone near me, handling me, trying to take off my clothes. Who is this person? A giant, savage, monstrous Kurd! Horror! If this murderer knows I am still alive, he will run his dagger through my heart and stop my breath. I try to control myself. I breathe as slowly as I can. I try to seem dead. He raises my head and lets it fall on the tiles. I bear the bitter pain silently. He moves my legs. He rolls my body, increasing the flow of blood. . . . In this way he succeeded in getting my coat, and now he was at my vest. He tried hard to take it off but not knowing how to unbutton it drew his dagger. O that moment! Would that dagger tear my heart?

The wife of the church sexton, Sister Mary, having escaped in some way from the hands of the enemy, was hiding in the next room, watching. As the Kurd drew his dagger to cut my vest, she, thinking he was about to stab me and unable to bear it, suddenly rushed upon him like a lioness and shouted, "Kurd, what are you doing!"

The Kurd, horrified, slunk back—who knows with what satanic superstition!—thinking perhaps that unseen evil spirits were persecuting him in the darkness. In a trembling voice he answered, "I'm not doing anything. I wanted this dead man's clothes. I couldn't untie his vest."

"Get back!" roared the voice. "I'll take it off and give it to you!"

The Kurd drew back like a cat. Sister Mary took off my vest and trousers and gave them to him. But coming closer he saw my underwear and asked for that too, and, taking it, disappeared.

I was naked, bloody, weak, lashed by the wind, my eyes blinded with blood, my breath faltering. Sister Mary—lone, forlorn, broken, in the darkness among the dead—suddenly let forth floods of tears and began a bitter lamentation: "O my dear pastor, you went away. O dear teacher, you too went away. And we widows and orphans are left. What can we do? Where can we go? We have no church, no school, no house, no food, no comforters. O God! God!"

Sister Mary was convinced I too was dead. When I knew that there was no one else in the room but her, I said softly, "Sister Mary." When she heard my voice, she knelt beside me and kissed my bloody forehead with the healing kiss of a mother. She was sobbing. "It is no time to cry," I said. "Help me." My heart was burning. "Bring me some water to quench this fire." Sister Mary quickly ran down the stairs, found a broken earthen dish, filled it with water and brought it to me. Then I said, "Try to take me to a safe place. If I remain here, the Turks and Kurds will come again and kill me." She ran out, and in a few minutes returned with another woman, Sister Sara. They had a dirty, shredded quilt in which they wrapped me, and these two angels, each holding one of my arms, made me stand on my feet. With heavy steps they led me down the stairs through the church yard, into another house, and up to a rooftop where about twenty Armenian women and girls, huddled together in the dark and cold, were bewailing the fate of their loved ones and their own hopelessness. They made me lie down and surrounded me.

Suddenly there was a tumult. People were climbing the stairs, coming on the rooftops with torches and lamps in their hands. Some of these fiends approached us, and when they saw only a group of helpless women, they were about to leave to search for other victims. But the blood-drunk eye of one of them saw my prostrate form in the midst of the group. The women were driven away from my side and I was stripped of my quilt.

Were these Turks moved by my wounded, naked condition? No, the Turk does not know the meaning of compassion, love, pity. When they saw that I was not dead, one of them drew his sword to stab me with it. When I cried aloud and pleaded and begged for mercy, they turned more fierce and growled, "*Gâvur gebermeli!* The infidel must die like a dog!"

An old woman, unable to bear my woeful cries, threw herself on me. She covered me with her body and said, "Kill me first and then this man. Have pity. It is enough. He is already dead."

The sword was withdrawn. The devils turned away. But the Turkish conscience had a sting in it. To leave before the giavoor (infidel) died was to be irreligious. One of them picked up a large stone and hurled it at my head. And now, certain that I had received the fatal blow, the group left, satisfied in heart and calm in conscience, fully expecting twice ten virgins in heaven to crown this meritorious act.

The women, feeling that my condition was hopeless, fled and left me alone. In the darkness, in the wind, in the cold, what was I to do? If I remained here I would be attacked again and killed. I had to escape. But was there enough strength in me? I turned my eyes toward heaven. Crying to God, I got on my feet and began to walk—no, I began to drive myself, to push and shove myself, sobbing, bending, stumbling, rolling, rising. Finally going down the stairs I passed through the yard and into the street. By chance I entered that same house to which the women had fled. This was an Armenian house adjacent to a Turkish agha's residence. On the floor was a little pile of wheat, and I stretched out on it to rest. This place too was attacked, but we managed to escape to the house of the agha, who received us and put us in a corner of his yard. We spent the last two hours of the night there, I prostrate on the ground, in a stupor.

On Sunday morning, November 3, 1895, the church bells were silent. The churches and schools, desecrated and plundered, lay in ruins. Pastors, priests, choristers, teachers, leaders, all were no more. The Armenian houses, robbed and empty, were as caves. Fifteen hundred men had been slaughtered, and those left alive were wounded and paralyzed. Girls were in the shame of their rape, mothers in the tears of their widowhood, orphaned children in wild bewilderment. The enslaved remnant was subject to nakedness and hunger, deprived of religion, honor, the very right to live.

But here and there some whose death had been decided upon beforehand, whose death warrant had been prepared, were still being hunted out. The Turks wanted to be sure that all these people had been destroyed. One of the names on this death list was mine. It had been discovered that the young Protestant teacher was not dead but missing.

This morning, a little after sunrise, a number of gendarmes and *başibozuk* surrounded the agha's house and threatened him, saying, "There are giavoors hidden here. Give them up!" The agha showed me and another young man to them, and we were immediately arrested. With their bayonets at our backs, they forced us into the street. When they recognized me, one of them said, "Hoja, we're taking you to the *konak*. The Armenian leaders, aghas, and educators are having a meeting there. They are waiting for you." They drove us on, but we were not going in the direction of the *konak*. I asked one of them, "Why are we going by this road?" He answered mockingly, "The road that leads to your meeting place is this one." Now it was clear they were going to kill us.

Walking ahead, we soon reached our meeting place. The sight

that met my eyes was a triple horror. All the Armenian leaders and religious heads, all those whose names were on the death list, were there. Slaughtered and soaked in kerosene, they were a burning hill of corpses. We two were pushed to the edge of this dreadful pile, and the Turk turned to me and said, "Here are your leaders! And here is your meeting place!" The guns were raised to shoot us.

In the very nick of time, when the command to shoot was about to be given, a Turkish ringleader turned the corner in front of us with his gang and, seeing us, shouted authoritatively, "Stop! Don't shoot!" He began to curse our executioners in the name of Allah and Mohammed, saying angrily, "These two have accepted Islam, and to kill them is to dishonor the Koran!" "But we know this man," they protested. "He is the Protestant teacher and it is impossible that he accept Islam." The leader bellowed threateningly, "I know he is a Moslem!" And he took us from that slaughterhouse, handed us over to two of his men, and commanded them to take us safely to the municipal prison.

Who was this person? I do not know. How he was moved to speak as he did to save our lives I do not know. Afterwards I tried to find him but was not successful. With his followers, this man had massacred many other Armenians. Why did he become our savior?

Why indeed others fell and God kept silent, I do not know. Why he allowed the head of James to be cut off (Acts 12:2), I do not know. I know only that the One who brought Peter out of prison was he (Acts 12:6-11).

In the prison were hundreds of Armenians—all of them wounded, crushed by the loss of their loved ones, bent under the horrors of the present, haunted by the nebulous terrors of the future. We remained here for four days, without food or water. There were no toilets, and we were obliged to use any corner we could find. The air was thick with filth, putrid, like a leprosarium. The pains of our wounds, the pangs of hunger, the fire of thirst, our desperate anxiety made this prison a veritable hell. If what is called hell is the continuation of such days, it is enough! There is no need of fire or brimstone there.

Among these people I was one of the most pitiable and

wretched, a soul abandoned and forlorn. I shall never forget a young man from Armenia, Hovhannes by name. He took off his coat and put it on me. He wrapped his girdle around my waist. He tied my wounds with his handkerchief. And always, putting my head on his knees, he made me rest and comforted me. One day a Turk brought a bowl of lentil soup to an Armenian friend of his. Soon it was devoured, and as the empty dish was being returned, I grabbed it, and rubbing my fingers here and there on the sides, I licked them greedily. When the air became unbearable, I would go to the door of the prison and pushing my nose in the cracks, breathe a little fresh air.

On the third day there was a rumor in the prison that all Armenians who denied Christianity and accepted the Moslem religion would be left alive, but those who refused would be killed. Each man was thinking what he should do. My own decision was certain. I would die.

On Thursday, November 7, the fifth day of our imprisonment, we were taken out and driven to the courtyard of a large inn. As we moved along in a file under guard, a crowd of Turkish women on the edge of the road, mocking and cursing us like frenzied macnads, screeched the unique convulsive shrill of the *zelgid*, the ancient battle cry of the women of Islam—the exultant *lu-lu-lu-lu* filled with the concentrated hate of the centuries. I said in my mind, as this scene impressed itself upon me, "Let Shimei's curse fall on David since the Lord hath hidden him. It may be that the Lord will look on mine affliction, and that the Lord will requite me good for his cursing this day" (II Samuel 16:11-12).

We reached the inn. Women and children engulfed us. They were weeping, wailing, choking, wild with despair. "In Rama was there a voice heard, lamentation, and weeping, and great mourning, Rachel weeping for her children, and would not be comforted, because they are not" (Matthew 2:18). One was saying, "Where is my father?" Another, "Where is my mother?" Still another, "Where is my child?" I think that even heaven does not know the heaviness of that day's suffering.

My stepbrothers' two young widows and four small orphans surrounded me, clung to me, wept and made me weep. They wanted their husbands and their fathers from me. I collected myself, struggling to preserve my moral strength. The hour to do my very best had come, to comfort not only my own but all the Armenian fragments, for I was left the sole leader and shepherd of this unhappy flock.

After remaining ten days in this inn, we were sent to our houses—no, to our caves, to dirt piles and bare floors. As I walked, slowly, I suddenly remembered that my father had buried fifty liras in a corner of our house. Surely that money would be a salvation in this terrible need. Leaving the widows and orphans behind, I ran to the house, but that corner, discovered somehow, had been dug up. There was nothing there but a mound. Yet I worshiped God and said, "I thank thee, O Heavenly Father; blessed be thy will. I had the rays of this one hope, and thou didst quench that too; thou hast cut away all ties from me. Thy purpose is good. I know that thou desirest me, having loosed all ties, to be bound to thee. Behold I am surrendered. Help me, my widows, and my orphans."

That mound became a Bethel for me. The door of heaven was opened to me, and my heart was filled with indescribable peace, a peace I could not have enjoyed had I possessed those pieces of gold.

Now the whole Armenian remnant was in consummate hardship. It was winter. The houses were without doors or windows. There was no bedding, or fuel, or clothes, or food. How was life possible? There was only one way—to beg, to go and open the palm. And of whom? Of our murderers, whose homes now were lavish with our own possessions.

We all scattered to the Turkish houses and began to beg. Women, girls, children were in the streets, here and there, begging bread. Oh, to beg is misery! To stretch out the hand and cry, "Help me for the love of God!" is an unmanly task. One day I was able to beg only four *mangïrlar*, about a penny. I bought some radishes with them, and the family supped on that that night.

Little by little tradesmen began their work again and were able to earn their daily bread. But those who had no trades, and the widows and orphans, were left abandoned and unprotected.

There was heavy snow everywhere. Traveling had ceased. Communication with the outside world was impossible. There was no help from anywhere. Who can describe our condition? At nights, famished, we lay down on the bare ground, in the dust and dirt, filthy with lice. We lived on our beggary. A hot meal was unknown to us. We often blessed the dead.

How did my terrible wounds heal? There was no physician, no apothecary, no medicament. There was no one to wash them and tie them up. I was my own physician; cold water was my medicament. I sewed a few pieces of old cloth together and, soaking them in cold water, washed my wounds. Repeated again and again, after three months this treatment healed me. All the other wounded treated themselves in like manner, and thus the healer was healed.

In the early spring of 1896 Mr. Sanders, the traveling missionary of the churches of Cilicia came from Aintab to Severek to witness the condition of the people. He was staying in an inn. Although it was very dangerous, I went to talk with him, still in my old, ragged clothes, worn-out shoes, and in a most filthy condition.

There were some gendarmes sitting near by, to keep an eye on him and find out what was going on between him and the Armenians. Fortunately, they did not understand any other language but Turkish, so he and I were able to speak freely in English.

During the course of the conversation Mr. Sanders mentioned that he had a little relief money for me but did not know how to give it to me without being seen by the gendarmes. I suggested that I remain with him that night and get the money from him after everyone was asleep.

"Good!" he said. He ordered a mattress and a quilt. We planned to sleep together and pass the money underneath the bedcovers. But one of the gendarmes went out and brought not one but two mattresses and two quilts!

It was just around this time that a Turk entered the room with a beautifully decorated and perfumed young boy, who sat down near Mr. Sanders. Mr. Sanders was puzzled, but I, being familiar with the perversity of the Turks, knew that this man took the boy around to be used for homosexual purposes and now he hoped to receive much money from Mr. Sanders for this "rare privilege."

Before letting Mr. Sanders understand the situation, I turned to the Turk and said, "This man is not the kind you are looking for. If he finds out why you're here, he'll be furious."

The Turk took the boy by the hand and rushed out.

Mr. Sanders got up to go to the toilet. It suddenly occurred to me that that was the best place to receive the money! I hurried after him, and when we were in the toilet together, I said, "Quick, the money!" and pocketed it. As I was returning I saw a gendarme coming toward us. But what was done was done. I had received the money. That night for the first time in a long while I slept a comfortable sleep on a soft mattress. With this money my people would again be able to eat with some regularity.

Gradually more money arrived from Aintab and Ourfa. The guardian angel of the Armenians living in Ourfa, Miss Shattuck, sent clothes, bedding, and money for food, and the people began to revive.

The years 1894, 1895, and 1896 were years of massacre, rape, and plunder. The order to massacre, issuing from Sultan Hamid, was given at different times for different places. During those years more than 300,000 Armenians perished by either massacre or starvation and disease. Wealth running up to the millions was destroyed. Thousands of orphans and widows were left destitute in misery.

To the people of America and England who, when they were cognizant of the wretched condition of the Armenians, sent their funds and great-hearted men and women to save a remnant from utter destruction, the Armenian nation is forever indebted.

The missionaries of Aintab appointed me pastor and director of relief, and for two years I worked in these capacities. The people loved me with a sincere love and respected me. They called me "the Moses of the Armenians." When my time came to depart, it was with great difficulty that I was able, through their tears and sobs, to give my last words of farewell.

In the early months, when the Gregorian church was not in a condition to perform its religious services, I invited all the Armenians to come to our place of prayer. All the services were held together until the Gregorian church was repaired and a new priest was sent from the city of Diyarbekir. The whole Gregorian congregation then moved with much joy to its own sanctuary.

In the summer of 1896, England's world-renowned professor, Dr. Rendel Harris, the benefactor and lover of Armenia, came to Severek with his greathearted Christian wife. He remained two days with us before directing his way toward the Armenian provinces. He spoke with me personally, learned my circumstances and future plans, and gave me some relief money. When in September of 1897 I returned to college, I learned that he had written the administration telling them he would be responsible for all my expenses both through college and through theological seminary. This news gave me great joy, for now I was able to go on with my studies with undivided energy.

In the autumn of 1897, two years after the massacre, Rev. Manoog Nigoghosian of Aintab came to Severek as pastor. I turned over all my work and accounts to him, and bidding farewell to all the Armenians I left for Aintab and in a few days I was at the college, to take up my work as a junior.

3

I PURPOSED, after completing my college course, to attend the theological seminary in Marash and to prepare for the ministry. Because the seminary received new students only once in three years, and a new term was to begin a year hence, it was necessary for me to take all the courses required for entrance during my junior year. This meant doubling my work and a consequent draining of my energies.

Persistently at my studies, I passed the first two months of this school year, but a pain began in my body and grew like thorns, choking my comfort and zeal. Dr. Shepard examined me and decided that I should undergo an operation. I was taken to the hospital and the operation was performed in the hope that two weeks later I would be able to resume my studies. But ironically, as a result, my blood was poisoned. A new, sharp pain began in my right arm. A second and then a third operation merely served to darken my hopes. The pain already in every part of my body, the pain of the wounds, and the successive pain of the daily change and treatment made life unendurable. I was melting and rotting under a severe temperature. Skeleton-like, for weeks I remained in bed, taking only liquid food. My suffering was so intense that I used to plead with the Lord to snap the cord of my miserable life and to take me unto himself. I could see the graveyard from my window. How often I turned my eyes to those silent stones and said in my heart, "Blessed are they who slumber there. They feel no pain."

After seven weeks of torture I began to lose consciousness and to babble deliriously. In the evening, when Dr. Shepard examined me once more, he turned, sad and disheartened, to Old Manoog Emmy, the night watchman standing beside him, and said, "There is no hope. In three hours Abraham will be dead."

This was the able Dr. Shepard's second hopeless verdict about me. He left the hospital and informed both the girls' seminary and the college that I had reached the crisis and that I would die. Unknown to each other, in these two institutions my friends gathered and prayed to God to preserve me.

But what did Old Manoog Emmy do? Rather than go home, sup, and then return, he thought it better, because I was in my last agony—and because there was a blizzard blowing—to wait at my bedside and carry my corpse to the basement, then go home unrestrained. He therefore went down to the coffin room, shouldered one of the coffins, and carried it up the stairs. Placing it before the door of my room, he came and stood next to my bed, watch in hand.

Months afterwards he told me his story: "After lowering the coffin, I came and stood by you. I would look now at my watch, then at your face. The hour was nearing eight, and taking my stomach into consideration, I was glad that the time was passing quickly. It was eight-thirty, and I said to myself, 'Only half an hour more!' But at nine, when I looked at you, you were still breathing and you did not seem as one about to give up his spirit. I became impatient. I was tired and hungry. However, I thought it better to wait yet a little longer. I waited till nine-thirty and ten. My anger was provoked! 'Whatever Dr. Shepard says must come to pass!' I said. 'Why in heaven's name is this boy disobedient? Why does he not die?' Finally it was eleven, but you were still alive. Convinced that you did not intend to die, I said to myself, '*Keyfi gitti!* Let him have his way! If he wants, let him die; if not, I don't give a damn! I'm dying of hunger!' And so I left you and went home."

Thus I struggled between life and death. And when in the

morning Dr. Shepard came to examine me, he was astonished, and said, "The danger is over! Praise the Lord! Abraham will live!"

I am sorry to say that Old Manoog Emmy had to shoulder the coffin a second time and take it back to its place. After that, whenever he saw me he used to say, "*Seni gidi seni! Salun gaç gaç günü!* You so and so! You fugitive from a coffin!"

In a few weeks I began to improve and soon left the hospital. Even with this interruption, I completed the year successfully. But the pain in my arm, severe or slight, continued for more than three years. Although I was not confined to bed, wherever I went, day and night, that pain, like a malicious spirit, ever followed me. I would sit through my classes restlessly and immediately after the lecture hurry to pour cold water on my arm to mitigate my suffering. But, comforted by the spirit of the Lord, I endured, and performed my daily tasks faithfully.

I spent the summer of 1898 at college. In the fall I learned that the theological seminary would not receive new students until the following year after all. Therefore I could remain in college another year and complete my course in the usual way. But as a senior I faced another ordeal.

During the two years after the massacre of 1895 that I had passed in Severek I had been engaged with the ministry and with the work of distributing relief. I had had a relief committee at that time and had kept records of all the relief work.

In the early part of 1899, when I was busy with my college studies, the Severek government searched the houses of the members of my committee. Besides writings and books, these officials found the relief records and, designating all this material as "politically dangerous," arrested the nine members of the committee and sent them to the prison in Diyarbekir. When cross-examination of the prisoners revealed that I had been the head of the committee, the government began to search for me so that the trial might proceed and all of us be sentenced together. The order was given from the vilayet of Diyarbekir to the mutessarif of Aintab to have me arrested immediately and sent under guard to the city of Diyarbekir. One day a gendarme, with a warrant in his hand, stood on the college campus asking the whereabouts of Abraham Hartunian.

The president of the college, Dr. Fuller, and Dr. Shepard went with the gendarme to the mutessarif. Abraham was their student and in the college, they said. "If it be possible, delay the matter a little while and wait and see what form it will take." My arrest was put off for about a month. But fear and anxiety now dogged my life. The order from Diyarbekir was repeated again and again, more and more emphatically. Nevertheless, my arrest being postponed in this and that way, I continued my studies and the school year ended. The last exercises took place. I received my diploma, under the threat of imprisonment, early in July, 1899.

The mutessarif wrote to the college president, "Let Abraham escape. When I am asked about him I will say he is nowhere to be found."

My friends advised me to escape to America. Everyone knew what imprisonment in Turkey meant. To incline in the direction of escape was natural and easy. On the other hand, there was a matter of conscience. My nine friends were in prison waiting for me. I was their leader. If I did not join them but escaped, more suspicion would be aroused about our work, and my friends' possible freedom would be endangered. If I were with them, perhaps I would secure their freedom. In any case, if we were to bear condemnation, we ought to bear it all together.

As I thought over these things, there was a storm in my brain. But I preferred to obey the voice of conscience and to take the path of duty, even though it was thorny and long. I decided to set out immediately for Diyarbekir to surrender myself to the government and so informed the missionaries. They were amazed. They in turn told the mutessarif, and he, grieving, said, "That young man is praiseworthy for this noble feeling of his. But the Turks do not know how to appreciate such nobility. They will kill him. Let him escape."

When the missionaries repeated that I had made a final decision, he said, "I trust such a man. I will not send him under guard. He is free. Let him go himself and surrender."

I made my preparations and was saying farewell to my friends when Mrs. Shepard met me and asked, "Where are you off to, Abraham?"

"To prison," I answered.

Petrified, she said, "God be with you. As a remembrance I give you the thirty-third verse of John 16: 'These things I have spoken unto you, that in me ye might have peace. In the world ye shall have tribulation: but be of good cheer; I have overcome the world.' "

Thus, after sunset one evening, I left Aintab, together with my muleteer, a woman with her child, a traveling Turkish gendarme, and the servant of Miss Shattuck of Ourfa, Hagopjan Eordoghlouian. We were on the Biredjik road. It led through places which were the abode of thieves and robbers and was exceedingly dangerous. We had traveled hardly two hours, a distance of about six miles from Aintab, when a terrifying voice came from the depths of the forest: "Stop and surrender!"

The gendarme began to tremble so hard that as he was trying to load his Martini rifle a few cartridges fell to the ground. We were indeed face to face with great danger, about to be robbed and even killed perhaps. But some genius now possessed Hagopjan, and he was changed into a Samson. He suddenly drove his mule in the direction of the voice and gun at the ready, roared like a lion, "Whoever you are, come out!"

There was no reply. Hagopjan, encouraged, shouted threateningly, "Come out right now, I say, or I'll shoot!"

A soft voice answered, "Our ass got lost and we wanted to know if you ran across it on the way. If you know nothing about it, go on. We want nothing else from you."

Hagopjan, now the master of the situation, commanded, "Come out right away!"

The robbers were defeated. One of them came up to Hagopjan, who seized him and made him stand next to him. Then turning to his accomplices he shouted, "All of you come here or I'll shoot this friend of yours!"

A second came out, holding a gun in his hand. Hagopjan snatched the gun away, emptied it in the air, and handed it to me. "Whoever is there, come out!" he yelled again. And the last one appeared. Hagopjan tied them together and ordered them to advance, threatening them with immediate death if they should move to the right or left or dare to look behind. In this way he made them walk for six hours, about eighteen miles, till we came to a village called Nizib, about three hours' distance from Biredjik. It was dawn. Because of the pleading of the robbers to be set free, Hagopjan did not turn them over to the government but returned their gun, admonished them, and put them on their way mortified.

From Nizib we journeyed to Biredjik, and from there to Ourfa. Here the good-hearted Miss Shattuck invited us for two days to her house. She paid our expenses for the rest of the trip to Diyarbekir. From Ourfa we went to an Armenian village called Garmouge and remained there for two days, then continued on to Der, where we spent a night in the house of the hospitable Protestant pastor. Finally we reached Diyarbekir.

Diyarbekir was a walled city. It was possible to enter it only by one of its four gates, each of which was always guarded by police and inspectors. We went in through the southern gate, called *Mardin Kapoosu.* I had hoped to avoid the eyes of the inspectors in order to visit friends and to glean particular information about my case before surrendering to the government. But hardly had I taken two steps inside the gate when the police surrounded me, arrested me, and opened my packages and searched them. Hearing my story, they would not allow me to go myself and surrender to the government but took me, like a notorious criminal, to police headquarters. I was locked up in a stable where another Armenian young man had been imprisoned for wounding someone in a fight over his sweetheart. My first act was to comfort this dejected young man. Then I lay down on a soft warm bed of horse manure and, being very weary, immediately fell asleep. Outward circumstances were grim, but my inner calm was complete.

Presently the chief of police sent for me. With Turkish savagery and in a thunderous voice he accused and cursed me; and handing me over to a gendarme, he ordered him to take me to prison where my friends had been confined for several months. I passed through the iron gates, which closed behind me and did not open for me again for thirteen months.

This was the central prison of the vilayet of Diyarbekir. It held nearly a thousand prisoners of different nationalities and languages, accused of one or another crime or perhaps already condemned. The particular place where my friends were confined and I was taken was a long narrow cell, with only one door and two windows, containing about seventy prisoners, each of whom had only enough space to mark his grave upon—hardly enough to stretch out and sleep untouched by others. The cell was always clouded with cigarette and coal smoke. It was filthy. Lice had freely built their nests on the prisoners and in the bedding. Millions of bedbugs swarmed everywhere. Riots, cursings, beatings, licentious speech, obscene Turkish songs, homosexual practices—these were the common happenings of the day. Hell was here.

My friends rejoiced to have me with them. I was the saddest of the group. The atmosphere of the prison had a disastrous effect upon me. Nevertheless, I had entered Gethsemane of my own will and had to bear all its terrors. I found my friends in wretched condition. With the four Turkish liras I had left I immediately began to provide the needs of all of us.

Through a friend who came to see me in the prison, I informed Miss Shattuck of our hardships, and she came quickly to our aid. She wrote to the English consul of Diyarbekir, asking him to take care of our needs at her own expense, and the consul, through his servant, sent us each week a small sum of money for our personal use.

Weeks and months rolled by but the court did not take up our case. No one outside was particularly concerned about us. Now and then we would get hold of a censored newspaper and pass our time reading it again and again. Sometimes the Armenian prisoners gathered to converse on spiritual topics. And now and then, we prayed and read the Bible.

Often wild fights and prison riots took place. Fists clenched and objects flew. Heads and bodies were torn and bloodied. At such times the safest place was the toilet—if it were possible to get there first, since many ran for it at the earliest sign of an outbreak.

To protect ourselves from the bites of the attacking bedbugs, densely omnipresent, we sewed large muslin bags. At night we took off all our clothes, got into these bags, and, tying the mouth from the inside, tried to sleep. To bear the suffocating, putrid air of the bags was easier than to be mercilessly eaten by the bedbugs.

Night and day, unceasingly, I heard the licentious Turkish songs. Many of them were impressed on my mind, and with an unintentional facility I memorized them.

After five months of imprisonment, one day a guard entered our cell and nailed on the wall above the bedding of my friends and myself a proclamation for each. Mine read: "This man is a revolutionary leader, and together with his committee he attempted to overthrow the Turkish Government, and in the name of Armenia, to snatch away part of this mighty land from the hand of the Empire; therefore, he is accused as one worthy to be punished with death; for which reason the trial will begin with the most punitive articles of the criminal law—according to the 54th and 58th articles, which decree death."

My whole body began to tremble. I took the paper in my hand and withdrawing to the darkest corner of the cell I knelt and poured out my heart to God. "Lord, it is true that the governor, the court, the judge, yea, all the officials, are my bitter enemies, and have determined even now to destroy me and my friends. But Lord, they are not able to raise a hand against thy servant if thou dost not permit. Wrestle thou against them for me and for my own, and save us from the claws of these beasts, from the cage of these lions."

It was time to pray, but it was time also to plan and to work. First of all, I had to inform Miss Shattuck, and through her the missionaries, of the present situation. But if I wrote a letter it would have to go through the censor, and certainly he would not pass it. Moreover, a letter of this nature would increase my crime and seal my doom. If I tried to smuggle a letter out, it would surely be discovered, since all who entered or left the prison were thoroughly searched, and I would thus not only endanger my own position but imperil someone else. But to keep silent and do nothing—this too was vain.

I found a pen, some ink, paper, and an envelope and wrote a detailed letter, telling Miss Shattuck everything. I sealed the letter, addressed it, and kept it ready on my person.

Early next day the servant appointed by the consul to bring us food from the market came to the prison, and I was called to take the victuals. There were iron bars between us, and I sat on one side speaking with the servant. Guards were standing near us. The inspectors were busy at their work. Leaning close to the servant I whispered, "I'm going to give you a letter. Give it to the consul."

The servant began to tremble. "That is impossible!" he said. "They will imprison me too!"

"Fear not," I answered. "Trust in God. Take this. Our lives will be saved by this letter, and you will be our savior." The servant took the letter in the utmost fear, quickly concealed it in his pocket, and was wondering how he might get out safely.

Suddenly something happened in that narrow place. There was a riot. All the guards began to run in the direction of the noise. Someone was being flogged. There was an uproar, shouting, confusion. "Quick!" I said to the servant. "Out the door!" Even before I spoke, he had jumped out in one leap and was gone. God had decided on our freedom.

After this event, every two weeks or every month we were taken to court, and our trial proceeded. Each time the same accusation was repeated and emphasized: "You are rebels and worthy of the death sentence."

On what evidence were they accusing us? They had the records of our relief distribution and one small piece of paper bearing my signature on which was written, "Lord, what wilt thou have me do? If Jesus were in my place, what would he do?"

The relief records "established" the fact that I had solicited a great deal of money and bought guns and ammunition and distributed them among the people. The sentence "Lord, what wilt thou have me do?" which they had translated into Turkish to read, "*Sahib, ne istersin ki ederim?*" "confirmed" the fact that I was asking the head of the revolutionary party, "My *Chief*, what is it you wish done?—to shoot, to massacre, to unfurl the flag of the revolution, to incite the people against the government and establish a free Armenia? I am ready. I await your order."

We did not have sufficient funds to hire a lawyer. The court had appointed one for us, but only for the sake of formality; he did not help us in the least. We had to defend ourselves. The truth is that I was the lawyer both for myself and for my friends. Daringly I defended our cause in every way, because it was just and because my conscience was clear. The members of the court and the spectators were amazed at my boldness.

The trial lasted many months. It was with the greatest difficulty that I finally convinced the court that that sentence is taken from the New Testament and is merely of spiritual and religious import. I took two Testaments to court, one in Armenian and one in Turkish, and opened them on the table. Handing the Turkish one to the secretary, I read the Armenian word for word. I impressed them with the fact that in truth this *is* the question of a revolutionary—not a political revolutionary but a moral and spiritual one, awaiting the command to rise up against sin. And they all kept silent.

The tenth month of our imprisonment passed. We did not know what Miss Shattuck was doing all this time. But we were sure she was working, and later we learned that our freedom was secured through her efforts.

When Miss Shattuck received my letter, she was deeply moved and immediately set out for Constantinople, where she called upon the American and English ambassadors. She explained the situation to them and requested their intervention. They in turn appealed to the Red Sultan of the time, Abdul Hamid II, and requested our release.

When Hamid heard my name, he said, "Just now I received a telegram from the governor of Diyarbekir. He writes that if Abraham Hartunian and his committee remain alive, the peace of these parts is imperiled."

The ambassadors insisted, "We know Abraham Hartunian and we are certain that all these accusations are fabricated and slanderous. We request his freedom as well as the freedom of the members of his committee."

Hamid, finding himself in a difficult position (because of the capitulations, since the committee had worked under the American and English relief boards), said, "Let the court give its verdict. I will later grant an *affe şahane*, a royal forgiveness, and set them free."

The ambassadors refused, objecting, "In that way Abraham and his committee will be considered guilty and then pardoned by you. Certain that they are all entirely guiltless in this matter, we request their acquittal."

The sultan finally yielded and promised to order the court to acquit us. The English ambassador then instructed his consul at Diyarbekir to look after our case, and one day the dragoman of the English consulate, Mr. Tovmas Mugerditchian, appeared in court. He was taking down all the proceedings. Day by day everything was reported by the consul to the ambassadors at Constantinople. Of course the court knew what this signified and already had received the sultan's order to acquit us. The presence of the dragoman encouraged us, but we knew nothing of these details.

Our case was in this state when one night I had a dream. In my dream my friends and I were standing on a boundless plain, looking into the far-off distances to which we were to walk. All at once the whole area was flooded and muddy and swampy. A voice said, "Go forward!" But we answered, "There is no place to step upon." The voice sounded again: "Behold the stepping-stones placed in the mud." And there indeed were the stones and we began to walk on them, and advanced far. But suddenly a mighty river appeared before us, impossible to cross. As we stood bewildered, the same voice spoke again: "Go forward! Pass by the bridge!" And lo, a sturdy bridge spanned that mighty river. We began to walk on it, but midway across, I turned and saw only six of my friends following me. Three were left behind and were not walking on the bridge.

The interpretation of this dream was immediate and clear. Up to this time I had passed through many trials, together with my friends, step by step. We were now nearing the final verdict. Seven of us would be declared guiltless and the other three would be condemned.

The last day of our trial arrived, and the dream came true. The court declared me and six of my friends guiltless and released us; but the other three were sentenced to three years of imprisonment.

It was required of us, according to Turkish policy, as the accused, to humble ourselves and with bowed heads to say, "May God give the *Padişah* long life. May he bless the members of the court. We are thankful for the just verdict given." If such an utterance as this was necessary, it was I who was to speak it. But I refused to express any such hypocrisy, and we all left the courtroom beneath the angry gaze of the judge and the frowns of the members of the court.

Three days after coming out of prison, well dressed and with a little money in my pocket, I went back to visit and comfort my three friends. I gave a little gift of money to some of the Turkish, Kurdish, and Arabic prisoners who had been friendly toward me. Then I gave small gifts of money to the guards, and last of all I visited the warden and gave him a gift also.

The warden smiled at me and, expressing the grief of his heart, said softly, "I was present at your trial a few days ago, and I noticed you deliberately offended all the members of the court and all those present. You did not express thanks and you did not pray for the sultan. We know that in your heart you hate us and the sultan. But at least for the sake of policy you should outwardly have expressed your thanks."

I answered, "For what things, my lord? Because I was innocent? Because I suffered for thirteen months? Because I experienced deprivations and terrors? Who shall pay for my losses during these thirteen months? You wanted me to be hypocritical and that is what I lack. Forgive me."

Now my major work was to visit the English consul, to thank him for his services and to beseech him to use his influence for the freedom of my three friends, who had been sentenced for some personal crimes trumped up against them. The consul promised his help, and I am happy to say that after one month they too were released.

For a few days I remained in Diyarbekir. On Sunday I

preached in the Armenian Evangelical Church of the city, and the church expressed the desire to keep me as pastor. I wrote to the missionaries of Aintab, but they were not willing, stating that it was necessary for me to enter the theological seminary.

4

I JOURNEYED from Diyarbekir to Severek, and from there to Ourfa, where about ten young people, on their way to college, joined me. We all had our *tezkere* (because Armenians were not permitted to travel even from one province to another without such passports). And we had no fear of running up against any trouble from the government. But when we passed from Ourfa to Biredjik and were about to cross the Euphrates River in boats, a gendarme approached us and began to pester us. I immediately understood that he was smelling out a bribe. Because I was sure of our *tezkere*, I stood out against him. This opposition irritated him, so he peevishly unloaded our donkeys and began to search our trunks. I had nothing that could have given rise to suspicion, but the students had many books and writings with them, and these were usually enough to brand an Armenian a political culprit and cause him to be thrown into prison. When I saw these books and writings, I began to fear. I had recently come out of prison and did not relish going back again. But to my great happiness, I soon discovered that this dutiful gendarme did not know how to read. Putting the books and writings to one side, he seized on a number of photographs and ordered me to go with him to the *kaymakam*, the civil governor of the district. I waited till all the students were safe on the other side of the river. It was after sunset when the gendarme and I reached the official building. The gendarme went into the *kaymakam*'s office and I remained outside. I could hear what was going on.

The gendarme gave the photographs to the governor and said, "I found these dangerous things on the giavoors."

The governor, who seemed to be a wise and good man, was much annoyed. *"Oğlan, sen zabïta mïsïn, yoksa eşek misin?* Man, are you a policeman or an ass? What is there in these photographs that you bring them to me? that you hinder these people from going on? Away! And let these people continue their way!"

The gendarme came out humiliated. I rejoined my friends. God had had mercy on me lest I have sorrow upon sorrow. We traveled on till we reached the American college in Aintab.

It was July of 1900 and there were only a few students in the college. For the rest of the summer I passed my time here, studying books on theology. In the third week of September I went from Aintab to Marash and was accepted into the theological seminary.

Since the other eleven students in the seminary had completed their first year, I was forced to take the courses of the present year with my classmates and also to cover the subjects of the previous year and pass examinations in them. My work was very difficult, but, struggling night and day, I fulfilled the requirements of my year's absence. In June, 1902, I was graduated and received my diploma. At last I was ready to work as a preacher.

During these two years in Marash I had intimate fellowship with the Armenian community of the city, with the three Evangelical churches, and with all the religious institutions and societies. I taught in the Sunday Schools and sometimes preached from the pulpits; the people loved me dearly.

It was in January, 1902, that I had the great happiness of meeting one of the teachers of the girls' college of Marash, Miss Shushan Kazanjian, a Christian woman, refined, capable, and noble in character. I revealed my love to her and she accepted me, and at the end of June, immediately after the closing of the school, our official engagement took place in the building of the girls' college.

In the latter part of June the annual conference of the Union of the Armenian Evangelical Churches of Cilicia took place in Marash. The present graduates of the seminary, according to constitutional requirement, were examined before the conference. We were questioned both about our belief and doctrine and about our Christian experience. Our examinations were satisfactory, and all of us received our license to preach.

Saying farewell to Marash, I left for Severek to begin my work. My fiancée went to Aintab to teach for another year in the girls' school there.

I acted as minister in my birthplace for two years and two months, from July, 1902, to September, 1904—alone the first year but with my wife the second. During this time the church work was very successful. The services were thronged. Gregorians and even Catholics and Syrians attended. The prayer meetings were inspired. As a result, in the spring of 1903 there was a spiritual awakening which continued for months. Each day, morning and evening revival services were held. Many repented and confessed, and former wrongs were compensated. The Lord's blessing was upon the people.

One such change of heart was indeed inspiring. There was a young man in the city who was such an evil, unruly vagabond that the people spontaneously called him *Sadana Avo*, Satan's Message. (His real name was Avedis, which in Armenian means "good news.") Having heard of our revival services, he came to church one day, with a number of like-spirited fellows, his purpose being to steal shoes (since those who attended the services, according to native custom, used to enter the church in their stockinged feet, leaving all the shoes lined up at the door).

When I saw this group come in, I was joyous, thinking they had come to be blessed by the service, unsuspecting that their object was theft. On this, their first visit, they listened attentively to the repentant and departed without stealing anything, since Avo told his friends, I later learned, that they should leave off thieving this once.

Next day the same group came back, knelt prudently with the rest, and saw and heard the works of revival. After a while Avo arose and, weeping, confessed that the previous day and this day too he had come for theft but had been moved by the spirit and knows that he is a sinner, that he repents and requests prayers for himself and for his group. Many prayers were offered for him.

The following day, a Bible in his hand, he came in and boldly confessed his salvation. Henceforth, he went through the streets of the city, from house to house, carrying the good news to all and leading them to the salvation of Jesus.

The people changed his name and called him *Hureshdag Avo,* Angel's Message!

During the annual conference of the Union of the Armenian Evangelical Churches of Cilicia in June, 1903, I went to Aintab both to take part in the meetings and to be married. On Friday, July 3, in the presence of more than four hundred guests and under the guidance and blessing of many pastors who had come to the conference, the wedding ceremony took place in the large hall of the college.

My beloved wife was born in the village of Yoghonoulouk, near Antioch in Syria, at the foot of Musa Dagh, on July 30, 1878. Her parents, Mr. Michael Kazanjian and Mrs. Heripsimeh Kazanjian, were devout Christians. She spent her first eleven years in her native village, receiving her primary education. Then she was accepted by the girls' school in Aintab, and immediately after graduation five years later was appointed an instructor in the same school, where she worked for four years. At twenty she was sent to the American girls' college of Constantinople as a student, and following two years of study there she was invited to the American girls' college of Marash as a teacher in 1900— the same year I entered the theological seminary. In 1902 she was engaged to me, and from 1902 to 1903 she served again as a teacher in the girls' school of Aintab. She married me in 1903. We remained two weeks in Aintab and then went to Severek to begin work together in the Lord's vineyard.

During the autumn of 1903 two wealthy British women, on their way toward the Armenian provinces, stopped in Severek.

While passing through Tarsus and Aintab they had heard about me from the missionaries, and one day at dusk a policeman came to my door to inform me that these ladies wished to see me. I knew that such interviews were exceedingly dangerous for the Armenians, but I could not refuse, since refusal would have created even more suspicion. Therefore I instructed my sexton to prepare two lamps, and together we went out of the parsonage to the center of the city, where a tent was pitched in the courtyard of a khan. The Britishers invited me in, and we began to converse in English. They asked me questions about the city, the churches, and the condition of the Armenians. I answered them. Then they gave me a letter written by a student from Tarsus, to be given to his mother. Putting the letter in my coat pocket I took my leave.

But when I had gone a little way from the tent, a policeman grabbed me and ordered, "Come along to the *konak!*" I knew what this meant. I would now be cross-examined and searched. If any written matter were found on me, I would immediately be marked a politically dangerous character and sent to prison. The eye fears what it has seen. I was afraid. I tried to bribe the policeman to let me go, but he was unyielding. My great fear was my pocket notebook, in which I had jotted down all kinds of things. Perhaps not one of these items was political, but the Turkish genius could have given a political turn to every word. Prison had terrified me. One verse from the Bible had cost me thirteen months of horror. I wanted desperately to destroy the notebook, to throw it away. But I could not.

Presently we came to a place where the policeman and I were alone. (I had previously sent the sexton home.) Perhaps I could escape. I decided to run back to the British women and beseech them to help me, to intercede. It was very dark as I leaped away. I could have outrun the policeman, who pursued me, shouting, "*Gâvur tutunuz!* Get the giavoor!" But suddenly some Turks came out of a coffeehouse and began to walk toward me. I could not have cut through them and escaped. So I turned back and surrendered to the policeman, and together we entered the *konak* which was very near by.

The hall was full of officials and gendarmes, all of them surly and evil. There was no way out of the cross-examination and search. More than the letter given me, the notebook in my pocket filled me with dread. I prayed silently, "Lord, help me. Let it come to pass that when they search me, thou wilt cause them to overlook my notebook."

Soon the questioning began, while two policemen searched me from head to foot. They looked in my hat and in my shoes. They put their hands in the left pocket of my coat and found the letter. But somehow they did not look into my right pocket where I had the notebook.

I remained in this place for four hours. They translated the letter and took it to the *kaymakam.* They deliberated for a long time, and finally, convinced that it was merely a filial letter, they let me go. It was midnight when I reached home.

I had hoped to stay in Severek for many years, but another upheaval was in store.

Two village chiefs ruling over the surroundings of the city— Ibrahim Pasha, an Arab, and Khalil Bey—became hostile to each other because of sectional disagreements. Murders and skirmishes led to open battle, pillaging of villages, and ruthless massacres. The Turks of the city were divided into two groups, each siding with one of these chiefs, and the peace both outside and inside the city was endangered. The Armenians, fearing for their lives, scattered to the cities of Diyarbekir, Chermoug, Chenkoush, and so on. More than half my congregation fled and the rest were planning to leave. The church board advised me to depart also.

On April 10, 1904, our first child, Harootune Albert, had been born. In September, when he was five months old, we set out with him for Aintab.

From Aintab I expected to go directly to Zeytoon to take up the ministry there. But the Second Church of Marash was without a pastor and asked me to work for them at least for one year. I accepted, and had much success. The church tried hard to keep me there permanently, but the missionaries did not consent. Therefore, in July, 1905, we left for Zeytoon, where, until the end of May, 1913, for eight years continuously, I worked as a minister.

The Walled City of Diyarbekir

Courtesy of the Hartunian Family

Dr. Shepard

Courtesy of Lemuel H. Kiretchjian

Central Turkey College

Bodies Prior to Burning

Courtesy of American Committee for the Independence of Armenia

No Place to Go

Courtesy of Armenian Democratic Liberal Organization

Abdul Hamid, the Great Assassin

Courtesy of the Hartunian Family

Abraham and Shushan Hartunian

Courtesy of Lemuel H. Kiretchjian

The City of Adana

5

DURING MY MINISTRY in Zeytoon the Armenian Evangelical
congregation rapidly increased. The old schools were re-
modeled. New ones were built. The sources of the church income were established, and paying real estate was bought. A new
parsonage was built, and the spirit of the evangelical work was
strengthened. In the strong spiritual awakening that resulted
many repented and the work of salvation was carried forward.

In order to improve the material welfare of the Armenians
of Zeytoon, I raised four to five thousand Turkish liras and with
this relief fund provided work for the people, supervising it myself through a committee which I appointed. We undertook to
lay out the streets of Zeytoon so that they would look clean and
attractive, to repair as far as possible the roads between Zeytoon
and Marash and Zeytoon and Albustan, to make passable the
places where travel was difficult, to build bridges, to remove
boulders. In this way, not only was work provided for the people, but their commerce both within and without the city was
facilitated. Widows and orphans and old folk and those unable
to work received relief directly.

The Armenian Gregorian community too poured out its
energy in full measure for enlightenment. Many schools were
built, and the people were on the happy road of progress.

During the years in Zeytoon we had four other children—Calvin, Helena, Rosalind, and Lydia. After living only six weeks, Calvin died of pneumonia. We were therefore a family of six, including our firstborn son, Albert, and three daughters.

In Zeytoon there were frequent disagreements among the aghas of the different sections. These now and then led to clashes and guerrilla attacks by one quarter on the other. There were rebellious movements, on a few occasions against the surrounding Moslem villages, but often against each other. Zeytoon at this time was a small free Armenia. The Turkish rule was nominal, and the Zeytoontsis could have lived in peace and freedom. But alas, neither freedom nor peace could last! The Armenian feared the Armenian. The Armenian violated the freedom of the Armenian. The strong oppressed the weak and persecuted him. Despite the fact that I was loved and respected, one day my own church was robbed.

After I had served as minister for two years, a great majority of my congregation desired to have me ordained. Applying to the Evangelical Union gathered in Marash in June, 1907, they received the approval of the conference. Thus on Sunday, July 7, a committee appointed by the Union ordained me in the presence of a large audience. Some of the members of the committee were Professor Sarkis Levonian, Rev. M. G. Papazian, Rev. G. Harootunian, and Rev. A. Shirajian. They placed their hands on my head and blessed me.

In August of 1908 Zeytoon officially celebrated the Declaration of Freedom of the Young Turks' Committee for Union and Progress. What shouting! What joy! Turks and Zeytoontsis embraced and kissed each other, proclaiming eternal love and fraternity! What great hopes! What bright dreams for the future! Yet even now the Turk was scheming for the annihilation of the Armenian people. Today the Armenian was hugging the very scorpion prepared to sting him. Zeytoon's destruction had been planned; Zeytoon's grave had been marked.

Hardly a year after the Declaration of Freedom the terrible massacre of Adana began—a massacre in which forty thousand Armenians were killed. Those who planned it were the Young Turks themselves. Their purpose was to put the blame on Sultan

44

Hamid so that they would have another pretext for overthrowing him.

The annual conference of the Evangelical Union was to take place during the week of April 11, 1909, in Adana. Pastors, ministers, delegates from every district would attend. I too was to be one of them, but divine Providence prevented me.

My wife—I do not know with what presentiment—stood out against my going. Indeed, she strongly insisted she would not let me go. And when, according to custom, the church took the matter up to decide whether to take part in the conference this year, the verdict was negative by a great majority. Just before this time the First Church of Marash was torn by internal dissensions, so the members of the board of that church invited me to work with them for a month and if possible to disentangle their difficulties. My own church being willing, I went to Marash, and I was there from Sunday, March 21, through Sunday, April 11. With the help of the Lord, my efforts were crowned and the difficulties removed.

On April 11, I administered the communion and prepared to return to Zeytoon to resume my work. The pastors and delegates from Marash set out for Adana on Monday, April 12, not knowing that they and their many consecrated friends were to be martyred. On April 13 the evil broke forth. The massacre of Adana and its surrounding villages had begun, and the blood of the Armenian was flowing everywhere amidst fire, plunder, and horror. On April 14, in the Church of Osmania, our able, select, holy prophets and apostles, professors, pastors, ministers, delegates, were burned to ashes. While the flames rose high, and their murderers mocked them and blasphemed the name of Jesus, the aged Rev. Giragos Jamgochian lifted his arms toward heaven and prayed, "O Father, forgive them for they know not what they do."

In Sighgetchid, in the vicinity of Hadjin, many honorable persons were butchered.

I, ignorant of all these things, and joyful at having performed my duty, left Marash on Friday afternoon, April 16, and was traveling toward Zeytoon. Hardly had I gone two hours' journey when some excited Zeytoontsis met me on their way to Ma-

45

rash. "What is happening in Marash?" they cried. "It is rumored there is massacre in the districts of Adana! Some Armenians from those parts have escaped! They are going to Zeytoon. They met us and gave us this evil news!"

I felt a chill and trembling in my body. But controlling myself, I said, "There is nothing in Marash, and I do not think the report is true." I spent that night in a village and the following day, Saturday, reached Zeytoon.

Zeytoon was a boiling caldron! The whole population was aroused. The Brave Lions were armed to the teeth, ready for battle. The Turkish general with his two thousand soldiers had withdrawn to the barracks and was keeping quiet. All the surrounding Moslem villages were in great fear, sensing that the fighters of Zeytoon would avenge the blood of their countrymen spilled in Adana.

The Braves of the city whose blood was now wild in their veins had immediately organized and raised an army. They wanted to attack the government building (already empty of its officials and police, who had fled to the barracks), to tear it down, to turn it inside out. They wanted to march on the barracks and kill the Turkish troops there, blow up the place, then swoop down on the surrounding Moslem villages and cities and even to go as far as Marash to revenge the blood of their brothers and sisters. Everything had been confirmed! The evil was real! The terrible massacre of Adana and its surroundings was an established fact! And there was more! This very day the massacre had begun in Marash, and at *Demircilerin çarşïsï*, the Bazaar of Blacksmiths, forty-six Armenians had been murdered with daggers or the crude, devilish blacksmith tools. Their corpses were still lying in the streets. Armenian messengers from Marash had reached Zeytoon before me and spread the news!

The ruling chiefs, notables, and religious leaders of Zeytoon came together. We advised the people to await the issue of the matter calmly and peacefully. If we allowed our fighters to attack the Turks and especially the barracks in this delicate time, they would give the Turks a pretext to annihilate all the Armenians of Marash and its surroundings. By keeping the peace, the Zeytoontsis preserved the lives of many of their countrymen.

We sent someone to the barracks to ask for an interview with the general. We were accepted, there was an exchange of opinion, mutual confidence returned. We persuaded the general to come back to Zeytoon, to send the officials back to their work to continue as usual. On Sunday, April 18, again at the barracks, we negotiated by wire with the officials of Marash, warning them that the peace of these parts would be assured only on condition that they guarantee the peace of Marash and its surroundings. They promised to keep the peace.

A few days later the overthrow of the Red Sultan was announced. Hearts were more serene, and our lives went on as before. But soon fresh lamentation broke out. Every year men from Zeytoon used to go to Adana during this season to work in the cotton fields. This year too they had gone and many had been killed. Those who returned brought joy to their families, but those who did not, sent sorrow and tears.

*   *   *

The next four years passed uneventfully and in the latter part of May, 1913, I moved to Marash with my family, to assume the pastorate of the First Church.

Let the reader bear in mind that it was one year before the World War that Providence led me from Zeytoon to Marash.

PART TWO

1914—1918

6

THE FIRST CHURCH OF MARASH had a congregation of more than fifteen hundred, about five hundred of whom were communicant members. The building itself was a magnificent structure on a beautiful, spacious campus, surrounded by three large school buildings which provided an education for nearly six hundred students. The church activities were many. We had a Y.M.C.A., a Ladies Aid Society, a Girls' Christian Endeavor, Sunday Schools with more than fifty classes, and a great choir. Everything was well organized. The prayer meetings were always inspired and edifying. Many attended the services, and antagonistic groups had united so that brotherhood and harmony prevailed. I was yoked to my work joyously and zealously, administering spiritual nourishment to my people, making my customary calls, conducting my individual interviews. My church was always crowded, and even Gregorians and Catholics used to come to services. From June 1, 1913, to the latter part of July, 1914, we passed a most successful and happy year. Our growth gave rise to the necessity of a high school for boys, and so on July 29, 1914, we began to remodel an old building and to add a new story to it in order to use it as a school. We did not know that on this day preparations were being made for the building of the World War.

Besides my own church, there were in Marash two other Armenian Evangelical churches. The Second Church, whose pastor was Rev. Siragan Aghbabian, had a congregation of twelve hundred; the Third Church, whose pastor was Rev. Aharon Shirajian, had a congregation of eight hundred. Then there were the American theological seminary; the girls' college; five German, English, and American orphanages, in which fifteen hundred Armenian orphans and widows were being cared for; a German hospital; and nearly thirty German, English, and American missionaries. Moreover, the Gregorian Armenians had six splendid churches, many grammar schools, and a large high school, and the Catholic Armenians had two most imposing churches.

More than forty thousand Armenians lived in Marash—wealthy, flourishing, well educated. And in the surrounding villages and towns, including Zeytoon, there was an equal number, totaling about eighty thousand Armenians in these parts. Marash was a busy, happy city. The Armenians were well settled and held high offices, even occupying important positions in the government. I felt very proud at this fortunate condition of my people.

In June, 1914, the annual conference of the Armenian Evangelical Union of the Churches of Cilicia was held in Aintab. That year I was president of the Union. Without knowing that the Great War would make this conference our last, would upheave our temples, wreck our firesides, and destroy our nation, we returned to our churches, inspired and full of hope.

Our last happy Sunday was August 2. War had been declared. The cold arms of death had been spread over humanity. The decisive hour of the fate of nations had struck. The opportunity to annihilate a subject people had broken the mist of the ages. The Turk was awake.

On Monday, August 3, from every corner proclamations were shouted. The rulers of Turkey had released stringent orders for everyone of military age: "All Moslems and non-Moslems must enlist. Any who do not respond will be shot."

The Turkish Army had to be mobilized for any eventuality. And within three months Turkey passed over to the Central Powers. All those of military age reported to the military centers and were enlisted. As in the whole world, so in our city and in the heart of the Armenian community peace and happiness had flown away, hopes had withered, and the former enthusiasm was no more.

Nevertheless, whatever terrors the future had, it was my duty to carry on my work with devotion, with patience, with steadfastness, and, even unto the end, to remain faithful to my calling. I continued all my church work as before, and I tried to comfort and encourage my flock. With great effort, and by the sacrifice of the people and their generosity, the building of the high school was completed. In the early part of October both the grammar schools and this high school were opened, and 650 students were enrolled. The other Protestant congregations and the Gregorian and Catholic communities similarly continued their church and school work.

On one hand, group after group, Armenian soldiers were being brought together and sent here and there with Moslem soldiers. Homes and churches were being deprived of their people. Weeping and wailing were heard everywhere. Business had practically stopped. The sources of income were drying up, and the people were desperate. On the other hand, the church and school work went on, and it was necessary to carry it on. Turkey too had entered the war. Oppression loomed on every side.

Marash became one of the military centers. Soldiers were brought from many places and sent to different fronts. Every day Turkish and Armenian women and children wept together as they hugged their men and bade them farewell. In truth these scenes were heartrending. But at least Moslem and non-Moslem were united and weeping together. They were consoling each other. They were comrades in tears. They had mutual sympathy. Would that it were always so! Alas, the picture changed, and soon the Armenian wept alone while the Turk laughed and mocked at the lamentation of his neighbor.

In this way 1914 came to an end. In comparison with the following years, what a blessed year it was! But we did not know it.

The terrible year of massacre, deportation, robbery, pillage, Gethsemane, crucifixion—the year of the annihilation of the Armenian people—1915 began.

53

Our last child was born to us on Thursday, February 11—the day commemorated by all Armenians in honor of brave General Vartan—and we called him Vartan, hoping that Providence would preserve him in this roaring furnace and use him, as General Vartan's brave descendant, for the vindication of Armenia's just right and cause.

The fear-pregnant month of February had passed, and the dread-begetting March had come. In other places the order to deport all Armenians had been given, and the evil plan was being carried out. The order had been given for our area too. It was to be put in effect first by deporting the Zeytoontsis.

General Fakri Pasha appeared in Zeytoon with two officers, Husein and Suleiman, and three thousand soldiers, well armed with guns, mountain artillery, and all kinds of military implements. His commission was to overcome Zeytoon and to open the road to deportation. Searching for a pretext, he soon found one: up to this time the people of Zeytoon had not given any soldiers. No one from Zeytoon had enlisted!

The general summoned the religious heads and aghas and commanded, "Within three hours all men of military age will report at the barracks. If not, I will strike and destroy the city."

The Zeytoontsis were willing, and pledged to exert their influence and to send the eligible men. With this promise they were set free. And in truth they tried to fulfill their promise. But the fighters of Zeytoon, instead of going to the barracks, grew stubborn and fled to the mountains. Finally the aghas succeeded in persuading about forty of the Braves to go and surrender. But instead of being placed in the army, these men were immediately disarmed, tied together, driven like cattle to Marash, and imprisoned as rebels.

And now about twenty fearless Zeytoontsis, at their head the Cholakian brothers, Aram Bey and Mesrob Bey, descended the mountains, armed, and entered St. Mary's Monastery, determined to fight against their enemy in his three-thousand-fold strength. Confident of crushing the Turks and liberating themselves and their beloved Zeytoon, they opened fire on the barracks, taking the offensive. David attacking Goliath! The general, befuddled with wrath by this boldness, ordered a discharge of cannons and a simultaneous attack on the monastery, cursing and bellowing for immediate annihilation! Of course he thought that in five or ten minutes he could finish these insolent mountaineers. But the battle lasted for twenty-four hours. And the general, seeing, with his own unbelieving eyes, three hundred of his soldiers stretched out between the monastery and the barracks, foamed at the mouth and became wild in his commands. He sputtered to Suleiman to advance his soldiers to the very doors of the monastery, and Suleiman, with drawn sword, took one step forward and rolled on the ground groaning, pierced through by the clear aim of a Brave!

The mountaineers fought until they were exhausted, until their last cartridge was fired. Then, in the darkness of night, knowing they could hold out no longer, they withdrew to the mountains, without the loss of one man, leaving the empty monastery to the Turkish soldiers, who burned it down.

In truth this bravery was praiseworthy, but it cost Zeytoon and Marash and the Armenians of the surrounding villages dear. From that day on, the Turkish government and the Turkish Army oppressed Zeytoon with increasing severity.

Enraged by the escape of the twenty mountaineers, the general had the bravest champion of Zeytoon arrested—Norashkar yan Nazaret Chavoosh. After spitting at him and mocking him in the barracks, and beating him till he was unconscious, he sent him to Marash to be cast into a dungeon on a high hill. After the bastinado and the unspeakable torture of daily having bits of flesh pulled from his body and the wounds sprinkled with salt and pepper, one day very near death he was wrapped in rags and brought out to be shown to the Turkish rabble. I saw him. A few days later, because of the stench which issued from his rotting flesh, an *Ittihat* Turk, the bestial apothecary Lootfi, under the guise of treatment poisoned him.

Successively other aghas were arrested and sent to the dungeon. The Turkish Army had surrounded Zeytoon. Her streets were filled with soldiers. Her strength was broken. The brave Zeytoontsis were at the mercy of the Turk, who knew not what mercy was.

Soon the deportation began. From April 4 to April 11, fifteen leading families of Zeytoon were brought to Marash and taken to the deserts to perish. One day a group of devout Christians, who called themselves Brethren of Christ, were brought from Zeytoon and hanged on a public thoroughfare. Until the ropes were passed around their necks and pulled, they kept on singing: "Coming home, coming home, never more to roam."

That year Easter fell on April 4. On Saturday, April 3, the prologue of annihilation drawn up against the Armenians of Marash was read. This very morning the Armenian quarters were surrounded by a chain of soldiers, and no one was able to get out. The houses of notables were put under special guard; among others, my own house was surrounded. A number of gendarmes entered, monster-like, and ordered us to remain where we were standing—I on one side, my wife near me, my elder children in their beds, my baby boy, Vartan, in his cradle. We were told that houses were being searched for guns, and that books and written matter were being examined. The investigating body would arrive in a short time.

This clearly meant deportation, death! And for all the members of my family! Oh God! That we were Armenians was proof enough that we were *evrak muzïre ve eczayi nâriye*, that we harbored "politically dangerous" writings and "firearms and ammunition." If they searched my library and writings, they would find enough to condemn me to immediate death. Especially when it was necessary to avenge the yet undried blood of Suleiman and the three hundred soldiers shot at Zeytoon! And who knows what was in my writings that could give "real" suspicion about my person?

Approaching one of the gendarmes humbly, with the low voice of a slave, I asked his grace, beseeching him to take pity on my crying child and allow my wife to go and nurse him. This privilege was granted. Then I said to my wife loudly, *"Hanïm, efendilere taam hazïrla!* Wife, prepare food for the gentlemen!"* I went and sat near the gendarmes. Soon the food was prepared and they ate and drank their coffee. A little later one of them said, "You can walk freely around the house until the investigating body arrives." I expressed my thanks and went into my library. One glance at my desk, and my head whirled. What "damning evidence" they could find there! It was not possible to examine everything. There was no time. What was I to do but resort to that custom I always used in times of crisis. I knelt down and prayed. "Father, prevent those men this day from coming to my house and making their search." Then with a calmer heart I returned to the gendarmes and waited.

But what was happening during these hours in other Armenian houses and institutions? Terror prevailed everywhere. The whole day passed in this way. At sunset two policemen came to our house and took the gendarmes away with them, saying, "Your house will not be searched today."

When they disappeared, I began to breathe freely. My heart full of gratitude, my lips glorified God as I hurried to my library: "Oh my God! At what an opportune time hast thou helped thy servant!" I found among my writings enough to destroy myself and my loved ones—"just" causes for our annihilation. Here was a photograph showing the aghas and champions of Zeytoon in military garb. And here was a long printed poem eulogizing the many victories of Zeytoon over the Turks, and the bravery shown! Finally, I discovered an account of mine written in 1911 when I was in Zeytoon and had streets and roads repaired. Sometimes in order to remove great rocks we had exploded them with powder bought by the pound. On the road between Zeytoon and Marash we had set up headquarters at a place called *Gureddin Kalasi*, the Fortress of Gureddin, where the work was headed by Cholakian Artin Agha, the father of the Cholakian brothers! In this account was written: "To Artin Agha at *Gureddin Kalasi* —so many *okkalar* of powder, date; so many *okkalar*, date; etc." —a long list of the times and amounts of powder sent. The Cholakian brothers, Aram Bey and Mesrob, with their comrades killed three hundred Turkish soldiers! And I had sent powder to their father, Artin Agha, at *Gureddin Kalasi!* Could a more "justifiable" cause than this be found for my destruction? I put all these in the fire and burned them. I cleaned the library thoroughly. And along with the smoke and flames, my thousand thanks were rising toward God.

There was no longer any safety for the Armenians of Marash. The days and weeks passed in continuous horror. On Ascension

Day, Thursday, May 13, Rev. Aharon Shirajian, with his whole family and ten other well-known families of the city, were arrested and deported—this was the prelude to the deportation of the Armenians of Marash. The Zeytoontsis were being deported caravan after caravan, group after group, brought to Marash and sent to distant slaughterhouses. When I saw the first great convoy—brave young men with drooping heads; women and children on foot, exhausted and weeping; nurslings screaming on their mothers' breasts—I was near to swooning. I sobbed like a child. My beloved Zeytoontsis were no more, and I would not be comforted.

Continuing thus, during April, May, June, and July, the deportation of Zeytoon was completed. Turkey's long-dreamt dream had come true. But hardly had Zeytoon been emptied when the deportation of the Armenians of Gurin, Albustan, and Yarpouz began. The people of Gurin had already suffered an attack by the Turks and Kurds on the road between Gurin and Marash. They had been robbed, their women raped, and the prettier ones snatched away; many had been massacred and the remnant was starving and wounded. O my God! I could not bear it! It was easier for me to be one of them and feel the same pain than to look on and see their suffering. Even the village folk around Marash were being driven out. Our own destruction was approaching. But first there was a small obstacle which had to be removed.

Two Armenian villages about five hours' journey from Marash—Fundejak and Derekeoy—were considered, after Zeytoon, Armenian strongholds. The people had been ordered to come to Marash in a body to surrender to the government. Of course they knew what this order signified, for at the very time it was given, the twenty mountaineers with their leaders, the Cholakian brothers, were in Fundejak and had spread the story of Zeytoon. Influenced by the presence of this group, and already hopeless and powerless, the Armenians of the surroundings had fled to Fundejak and determined to rebel. Having disposed of about sixty Turks living in the village, they were ready to fight for their lives.

On Wednesday, July 28, 1915, some gendarmes came and led

the Armenian religious heads, myself among others, and a few Armenian aghas to the parlor of the mutessarif. All of us were pale in countenance and seemed half dead. With trembling lips we entered the room, where the high-ranking civil officials and military heads were gathered. Their purpose was soon made clear. The government was ordering us to go to Fundejak to persuade the Armenians there to disarm and surrender! What were we to answer? It was impossible to refuse. So we accepted the commission—but what a delicate office! And what a heavy responsibility! If we succeeded in bringing them to obedience, we would have betrayed our children to murderers with our own hands. If we were not able to persuade them, we would be regarded as participants in their rebellion. But whatever the issue, there was no other way, and those who were chosen had to go. This difficult task was placed upon two priests, Der Sahag Der Bedrossian and Der Arsen Der Hovhannessian, and upon the pastor A. H. Hartunian.

The next day we three, under the protection of gendarmes, were put on our way. Passing through hundreds of Turkish *çete* and *başïbozuk*, we were led toward Fundejak. After resting on a hill for the night, on Friday morning we reached a mountain overlooking the village, where Turkish soldiers and an officer had encamped. The officer received us with great courtesy and respect, and we spent that day on the mountain while field glasses in hands, he observed the activities of the Fundejaktsis, who were throwing up barricades at strategic points. Now and then he would hand the field glasses to us, to show us what the "rebels" were doing. Cunningly he was striving to persuade us sincerely to attempt to induce the people of Fundejak to surrender.

On Saturday morning, July 31, we were ordered to descend the mountain and enter the village. Since both sides had now opened fire, and probably we would have been shot immediately if we had advanced, we requested a cessation of the firing. Signals were exchanged, and holding a white flag we went down the mountainside and reached the village safely. There, beside still waters, beneath the shade of trees, we rested. The village mukhtar, the aghas, the Cholakian brothers, and their brave Zeytoontsis, all armed to the teeth, surrounded us. We informed them of the danger; already three thousand soldiers had set out from Adana under the generalship of the military vali, Jemal Bey, to strike at Fundejak. But despite these warnings they unanimously answered, "We choose to fight and die, on the banks of this stream, under the shade of these trees, rather than be driven out to the deserts by the lash of the merciless Turk, there to rot in torture."

Their choice was a noble one. Indeed, we ourselves told them to fight. And not wishing to stay longer, we were about to return when some of the Braves threatened us, demanding that we remain with them. But when we made them understand that such a course would be very dangerous to our families and to all the Armenians of Marash, they softened and allowed us to leave. We blessed them in farewell, went back to the Turkish encampment, and related the details of our mission to the officer, whose former courtesy and respect were now removed by our failure. On the same day, again under the protection of gendarmes, we returned to Marash and presented our report to the governor, who was exceedingly displeased and treated us very coldly. Then we dispersed to our houses safely, but exhausted in body, depressed in mind, and hopeless in spirit—living but dead. From moment to moment we awaited the ill news of the destruction of Fundejak and the slaughter of the Armenians there. And in the evening the three thousand troops with all military preparations surrounded the village.

Sunday, August 1—the first anniversary of the beginning of the Great War—brought destruction for Fundejak and calamity for the Armenians of Marash. There were hardly fifteen hundred Armenians in Fundejak, in large part women, children, and old folk. The number of those able to fight did not exceed three hundred. It was against a mighty strength that they struggled. The three thousand troops, under the command of their general, had gripped the village in a military chain and advanced continually, narrowing their circle and firing from every side, while bombs roared from the mountains.

The Armenian Braves fought miraculously. Turkish soldiers fell to the ground on all sides. Again the omnipresent Cholakian mountaineers were overthrowing the Turkish soldiers, scorning fear and death. Finally the troops neared the village. Although the Turkish soldiers fell continuously, yet obedient to the command of their general they advanced until they could set the village on fire from every side. After a struggle of twenty-four hours, and a prodigious defense, Fundejak was occupied and burning. The smoke and flying ashes, like thick clouds, rose toward the sky and were clearly visible to us in Marash.

It was no longer possible to resist. The people, forced out by the flames, surrendered to the troops. The Cholakian brothers and their Braves made a last defense, then broke through the Turkish cordon and escaped. All the other men were captured by the soldiers and tied together. The women and children were herded in a field to be deported to unknown slaughterhouses. Some of the men were shot immediately. The rest were brought to Marash and cast in dungeons, later to be shot in the presence and to the joy of the Turkish rabble. More than five hundred Turkish soldiers had fallen, and their deaths had to be avenged!

A most horrible week had now begun. The government recognized me as the religious head of the Armenian Evangelical community of the city. Besides bearing my personal burdens, and those of my family and church, I had to carry also the burden of the other two Evangelical congregations, and in truth the woes of all the Armenians of Marash, because I was the intermediary with the government. In such a time as this, it was not easy to shoulder all Armenia's fears and groans, her terrors, her pains, her needs and dishonors; to comfort and encourage the wounded, the disconsolate, the hopeless; to wipe away the tears of orphans and widows. The common mortal could not have fulfilled this office if God had not come to his aid.

On Monday, Tuesday, and Wednesday, August 2, 3, and 4, I was with the governor constantly, trying to give the women and children of Fundejak who were being deported a little help. A number of pack animals, some food, some coverings were sent from Marash, and I am sure that from Fundejak to Aintab they had a reasonably comfortable journey. But after that, what happened in Biredjik, in Ras-ul-Ain, in Der-el-Zor, God knows and I know too. The Armenians of Fundejak were annihilated.

*　　*　　*

I desire to make an acknowledgment here. Both at this time and for two years more there was in Marash a governor by the name of Ismayale Kemal Pasha. Conscientious, kind, and justice-loving, this man was never in sympathy with the perpetrators of the crimes against my people. He tried by every possible means to save us and always was friendly toward us. Whatever evil befell the Armenians through him as a means did not issue from his person but from the strict orders sent out from Constantinople and from the pressure placed upon him by the Young Turks' Committee for Union and Progress of Marash. As many Armenians as were saved owe their lives to his mercy and soundness of character. This pasha was especially friendly to me. He would call me to him privately and inform me of the situation, pointing out the difficulties. His position was most trying and often pathetic. Many times he showed me the telegrams sent from Constantinople by Talaat Bey and Enver Pasha. These telegrams ordered the massacres, forcing all high officials to deport the Armenians from their cities, to confiscate their possessions, and to murder them in unknown and distant places without any remorse —men, women, the old, the young, from babes in the cradles to enfeebled old men—considering it a duty for patriotism and nationalism. Ismayale Pasha used to turn to me and ask pleadingly, "Badveli (Pastor), what shall I do?" The name of Mr. Henry Morgenthau, the American ambassador to Turkey during the Armenian terrors, especially should be mentioned. This magnanimous and brave soul, both in the name of the American government and also in his individual capacity, did his very best to keep the Turks back from their murderous path and to lessen the suffering of the Armenians. "If I am to suffer martyrdom," he wrote, "I can think of no better cause in which to be sacrificed. In fact, I would welcome it, for I can think of no greater honour than to be recalled because I, a Jew, have been exerting all my powers to save the lives of hundreds of thousands of Christians"

(*Ambassador Morgenthau's Story*, Doubleday, Page & Company, 1919, p. 379).

* * *

On Thursday, August 5, after the Fundejaktsis had been deported and their village turned to ashes, the corpses of the Turkish soldiers buried, and those of the Armenians strewn out on the plains for wild beasts and vultures, the general of the Turkish Army and military governor of Adana, Jemal Pasha, entered Marash victorious. For the Turks it was a day of *bayram;* for the Armenians, a day of mourning. We religious heads hastened to the Pasha to humble ourselves before him, kiss his bloody hands, bid him welcome, and beg his grace and pity for the Armenians of Marash. What a proud, crabbed, bestial man he was! He began to speak, and his subject was the Armenians and their ingratitude, their unforgivable sin. Receiving from him no glimmer of hope, we returned to our houses with heavier fears.

That same day, about six o'clock in the evening, we held our weekly prayer meeting. Rev. Hagop Yeranian, the pastor of Afion Kara-Hissar, who had been deported from there to Marash and who collapsed later in the last conflagration of Smyrna, was leading us. The meeting nearly half over, suddenly the school buildings and the campus were filled with soldiers, the new troops occupying the important Armenian centers. We all arose. Rev. Yeranian chanted the *Der Oghormia,* "Have Mercy, Lord," and we joined him. Then, receiving his blessing, we departed to our houses.

On August 6 a terrible order was given: "All Armenians must surrender to the government whatever firearms they have; if a gun is found anywhere during the ensuing search, the owner will be shot instantly." At the same time preparations were being made to deport us the very next day.

Saturday, August 7, had come! The day of hell! The prison gates were thrown open, and about a hundred captives from Zeytoon and Fundejak were brought out. Chained together, they were led to their slaughter through the streets, to the shouts and joyous outcries of the Turks. Some were hanged from scaffolds in the populous centers of the city. The rest were driven to the foot of Mount Aghur and there were shot in the presence of a great multitude. Gendarmes went among them after the first shooting and crushed the skulls of those who were still alive. This terrible scene was witnessed by a German missionary, the good Mr. Speaker. When the Turks saw him standing there, they shouted, *"Yaşasïn Türkiye! Yaşasïn Almanya!* Long live Turkey! Long live Germany!" And Mr. Speaker answered, *"Bu bisuçlarïn kanï ne Türkiye'yi ne de Almanya'yï yaşadïr.* The blood of these innocent can sustain neither Turkey nor Germany."

I was at his bedside when Mr. Speaker died a few weeks later, unable to bear these injustices. The dagger in the breast of the Armenian had pierced him too, just as it did the missionary of Aintab, Dr. Shepard, who died in his home, his heart crushed by the suffering of the Armenians in Ourfa.

These hundred corpses were still lying on the ground when suddenly hell's harbingers ran through the streets shouting, "All Armenian men, seventeen years old and above, must go out of the city and gather in the Field of Marash, to be deported; those who disobey will be shot."

As I now recall that day, there is a trembling in my body. The human mind is unable to bear such heaviness. My pen cannot describe the horrors. Confusion! Chaos! Woe! Wailing! Weeping! The father kissed his wife and children and departed, sobbing, encrazed. The son kissed his mother, his old father, his small sisters and brothers, and departed. Those who went and those who remained sobbed. Many left with no preparation, with only the clothes on their backs, the shoes on their feet, lacking money, lacking food, some without even seeing their loved ones. Already thousands of men had gathered in the appointed place, and like madmen, others were joining them.

The scene was so dreadful that even the hardened Turkish heart could not stand it, and a second order was given: "Those who have gone, have gone; the rest may remain. Let them not go."

Thus the thousands who had given themselves over to the hands of the bloodthirsty gendarmes were driven out to the desert slaughterhouses. The remainder, crushed, pale, hopeless, were left in the city to await their turn. It was no more a secret that the annihilation of the nation had been determined.

How can I describe my mental anguish, the agonies of my heart, my emotions! The scenes of that day had bereft me of mind and strength and will. But in this thrice-exhausted condition I still had to comfort my family, to encourage my remaining people, and to do my possible best. I had to visit houses to give consolation. I had to appeal to the governor and to other officials —bowing before them, to beg and cry for mercy for the Armenians. And I too was waiting to walk the road of deportation.

I had all the furnishings of my house packed in boxes and bundles and sent to the American buildings. For the journey I brought together the absolutely necessary things: a tent, water jugs, a cradle! All the money I had was eight liras. How was it possible to travel with my wife and five small children? My God! The very thought makes me shudder!

On Sunday, August 8, the subject for our thought at church was the crucifixion. The nation was on the cross.

From this day on, the work of deportation was carried out systematically. Every day new lists were prepared, and successively the convoys were put on their way. Everyone knew that in a little while his turn would come. There was not a glimmer of hope. Indeed the bitter scenes daily enacted in the city rendered the people willing to go out and face death as soon as possible. Innocent Armenians by the dozens were hanged from scaffolds in different sections of the city, and their corpses dangling in the air wrought horror upon the people. On different days and in different places nearly five hundred Armenians were either shot or hanged.

On Sunday, August 15, the subject of our spiritual meditation was the burial of Jesus. My people were being entombed.

The list of deportees on Thursday, August 19, included the names of the Protestant families. More than eight hundred Protestants were forced out of their houses and, with over a thousand Gregorians and Catholics, driven out of the city. I was running here and there, trying to see for the last time the sheep and the lambs of my flock. Oh, these heartbreaking interviews! Surprisingly enough, the Turks seemed in a great hurry, supplying the people with mules, donkeys, and horses. The caravan got under way.

With bowed head, I was returning to my house when a policeman accosted me: "The mutessarif summons you immediately." It was evening, near sunset. Why should I be sent for at this time? The mutessarif was alone in his office. He smiled at me and said, "I wish to give you the good news that, according to an order from Constantinople, the Protestants, after today, are exempt from deportation."

When I heard these words, my emotions clashed. I was bewildered. Although happy that at least some Armenians were going to survive, I was sad that just today more then eight hundred who could have been benefited by this order (since I learned that it had reached the mutessarif in the morning) had been sent away.

I did not know what to say. I bowed before the governor, stammered my thanks—and then, inspired by a mortal boldness, I said, "My lord, I want my people."

"That is impossible," he said. "They have already gone. The remainder have been saved and that is sufficient."

I began to sob. I pleaded. "Lord, give me back my flock!"

For half an hour a moral battle raged in that room. Kissing the governor's hand I said to him, "The opportunity to become the savior of more than eight hundred souls has been offered my lord. I do not desire my lord to let it by."

"This will be the cause of both your death and mine. Let us leave it alone," he said.

"Fear not!" I answered. "The God of life and death will save both you and me."

Finally Ismayale Kemal Pasha pitied, and his good heart relented. I requested an order directing the commissar to supply me with gendarmes that I might go and overtake the deportees and return my flock to its fold. I received the order and, bowing low, withdrew. I ran breathless to the outskirts of the city to find the commissar who was supervising the deportations and presented my order to him. Darkness was closing in. When he read it he was furious. He glared at me. "This is absurd!" he said. "Why do you meddle into the affairs of the government! Are deportees ever returned! This is impossible!"

I answered, "Your honor, the governor has commanded, and his command must be obeyed."

He immediately got to his feet, angrily ordered the gendarmes to put the rest of the victims on their way, and as the gendarmes lashed away and shoved with the butts of their guns he headed toward the governor's house. I followed him. What was a giavoor doing in this Turkish pack? The governor listened to both of us. The commissar kept insisting, "There are only a few Protestants! I can't separate them!" And I was imploring, "My life on it! Eight hundred Protestants have gone, and they must come back according to the order from Constantinople!"

Finally the governor turned to the commissar and said, "Carry out my orders immediately!"

We left the house, and a moment later the commissar gnashed his teeth at me, saying, "You will pay for this with your life!"

I went to the *konak*. I sent word to my wife, informing her of my mission and of my absence that night. In a little while some gendarmes came, and, mounting swift horses, we galloped out of the city, into the darkness of night, into the shadow of death. In three hours we reached the encampment of the convoy.

The deportees had traveled only a few hours. They were still near the city. Not yet had begun the separation of the women fated for rape. Not yet had begun the herding of the men to be robbed and massacred. Not yet had begun the abandonment of the old folk and children on the roadsides, to rot and perish! This was the mere prologue to horror. The deportees, exhausted, were stretched out on the ground like tired sheep. The heart-rending wails of the children were piercing the air. The women were sobbing. The wild gendarmes, like wolves, were watching them from every side.

"Badveli has come to take the Protestants back!" Oh, the currents of opposite feelings! Those to be freed were joyous. The rest were anguished because they were deprived of the escape offered by this opportunity. But in this world, whichever way you turn, no matter what you do, there is nothing that can satisfy the heart—thorns and thistles, pain and grief, weeping and wailing!

That night I stayed with the convoy. The next day I received my flock to my side. A new separation, a new weeping, a new wailing! One to one side and another to another side! Finally the bonds of love were again severed, and I, taking eight hundred Protestants and about two hundred Catholics and Gregorians, went back to the city and settled them in their homes.

All the Turks, especially the *Ittihat*, were exceedingly displeased by this occurrence. They began to murmur against the governor. I became their most hated enemy. In order to appease their bestial will, they invented a diabolic ruse: "Dangerous characters are exceptions and must be deported."

Thus a number of rich and influential Protestants—about twenty families, or nearly a hundred individuals—were sent back. But the remaining seven hundred who would have perished in the fields of Der-el-Zor were saved, and of these about three hundred are living today (1939) and remember that rescue.

*   *   *

Sometimes there would be an interim of a few weeks, after which the deportations would resume. From week to week, from month to month, the number of my people was decreasing. Among those who were left, the great majority were old folk, women, and children. Our church and school buildings were being occupied. Our schools were being used now as schools for the Turkish children. The belongings of the deportees had been confiscated, their houses occupied by the Turks. No Armenian was able to travel at will. All our fields, vineyards, and gardens were in the hands of the Turks. As a people we were subject to the curses of the twenty-eighth chapter of Deuteronomy: "Cursed shalt thou be in the city, and cursed shalt thou be in the field. Cursed shall be thy basket and thy store. Cursed shall be the fruit of thy body, and the fruit of thy land, the increase of thy kine, and the flocks of thy sheep. Cursed shalt thou be when thou comest in, and cursed shalt thou be when thou goest out."

With continuing woes and fears, the cursed year of 1915 came to an end, and 1916 began, to complete whatever 1915 had left undone.

Because the house in which we were living was a good building, it was not considered a proper dwelling for a giavoor. When it was snatched away from us and given to a Turkish officer, we were forced to occupy a few rooms in one of the buildings of my church campus. The Armenians no longer had any right to education, and the campus was now filled with hundreds of Turkish children. In one of the school buildings one floor had been occupied by the officer in charge of the deportations. His hellish crew was carrying on its work of destruction against my people in my own building, before my eyes. Life in such an atmosphere, day after day, was unendurably bitter.

It is necessary to bear in mind that the Armenian population of the city was day by day being reduced in numbers, and the hardships of the remnant were ever growing. The most terrible and unbearable thing was that this situation had no end, no beginning, no limit. Every individual, each family, from second to second, was in horrid expectation of deportation, imprisonment, or immediate death. Every few days new corpses could be seen dangling from scaffolds. This was the life we were living. As here, so in every part of Turkey the condition of the Armenian was thus, and even more evil and unbearable.

One day in February a policeman came and led me to the *konak.* There I found the members of the committee for the enlistment of soldiers. They questioned me about a number of Armenian men of military age, many of whom I did not know. I naturally answered, "I know nothing," and they wrote down what I said and made me sign it.

In a few weeks another policeman came with a warrant for my arrest. I was taken again to the *konak,* and immediately put under guard. A long-drawn-out cross-examination took place. A few weeks previously I had, by my signature, testified to the fact that "The following Armenian men whose names appear on the military list are unknown to me. I do not know their whereabouts." Yet every one of these men, according to the committee, was in Marash at the time I had made that statement. I had therefore deliberately given false testimony about them and thus kept them from military service. I was a detriment to the very existence of the Turkish nation! What a great and terrible crime! Could a more "fit" and "just" cause than this be found for my deportation and death?

I used every means to defend myself, but it was all to no avail. The Committee for Union and Progress, still furious because I had brought back the Protestants, had at last smelled out the pretext to satisfy their monstrous desire upon me.

For five hours I waited under guard. What could I do? Nothing but look up to heaven, to the Almighty, and ask that he come to the aid of his servant. I had given my cause over to him, and though my body was trembling, my heart and spirit were calm.

Just in these hours, more than my personal grief, a heavier care and anguish overburdened me: Driven from far distances and scattered in the Turkish and Kurdish villages around Marash, some of the many Armenian women, surfeited by the hardships to which they were daily subjected—and who knows what inhuman rapes!—had dared to come to Marash on foot, in the hope that at least here they would get some relief and be able to protect themselves in secret corners. Entering the city, they had been captured by the police and now were being driven along under the blows of heavy fists, accused as traitors and defrauders. Preparations were being made to return them to the villages whence they had fled. These young, beautiful women were beseeching that they be granted the mercy to remain, and they were being roughly refused. Already many like them had been massacred. Was it that even these, after sating the bestial Turkish lust, were to be massacred? This dreadful scene made me forget my own danger. They were close to me, yet I could not speak one word of comfort to them. What is the Armenian going to do with comfort?

A trumped-up legal accusation had been written against me: I was a most dangerous character to the welfare of the empire. The very existence of the government was threatened by the faithlessness and treachery of the religious head of the Protestant church. Therefore, for his treachery he must be punished by either death or deportation.

This paper was sent to all the high officials in the different government circles, and each one, with malicious pleasure, placed his seal upon it. Finally it was presented to the mutessarif for his ratification, which would have immediately placed me at the mercy of the military court, signifying that the final word had been given for my destruction. This was exactly the expectation of all the Turkish officials. What a delicate situation! What a critical moment!

Ismayale Kemal Pasha, who knew me well and whose heart was inclined toward me, received the accusation, read it, and, knowing that the inventor of this base injustice was the envy of the officials and the members of *Ittihat*, instead of sealing the document in the desired fashion and forwarding it to the chief of police, directed it to the court. Summoning the prosecuting attorney and the judge to him, he explained the situation and ordered them to call me to court, to examine the accusation, and to acquit me.

The trial took place indeed. After long investigation, it was established that every one of the Armenian young men whom I had testified I did not know were in the city serving out their terms of military service for the government. To the shame of all the officials and to my great happiness, I was acquitted and returned home, unable to fathom how in such a time, in such circumstances, an Armenian could have a just trial and freedom. With my whole family I glorified God and his miraculous power.

On April 9, after church service, I called a short meeting of the board. We were all depressed. Although the religious work was being carried forward within the bounds of possibility, nevertheless, our bodies, minds, and spirits were revolting, saying, "No longer is it possible to endure!"

The five-year-old son of one of the members of the board was climbing about the platform, wandering here and there. He had gone under the pulpit and presently emerged with a package in his small hands. We opened it, wonderingly. It was a collection of letters—but what letters! They were addressed to the conference of the Cilician Union, sent by the Armenian Evangelical Churches of Cilicia! What letters for the present time: *Cilicia, Union, conference!* There was no need to examine the contents. Only this much was enough to condemn myself, my family, my church, my whole congregation!

Thanks to God that the church building had not yet been searched. And a thousand praises that this small angel had brought to light this curse sufficient for our destruction. God, even by the play of children, has great works to perform and histories to write. I hurried home and threw the letters in the fire. With joy I watched the bright flames which perhaps would have burned my whole flock.

Just a short time later the church *was* searched. If on that day the child had not found the package, and it had passed into the hands of the *Ittihat,* what the result would have been is not hard to imagine! On Tuesday morning I had just got out of bed when the police, gendarmes, *yüzbaşilar,* officials, crafsmen, and *başibozuk,* with guns, swords, axes, and all kinds of tools, surrounded my church. Had they come to massacre us? No, they had come to search the building. The vengeful Young Turks had plotted against me thus: Badveli has concealed guns, war implements, and dangerous documents in his church."

I brought the key and opened the door. Immediately they rushed in and began their search. They nosed around for hours. They dug up many places on the ground with pickaxes. They ripped off boards from the walls, overturned the furniture, smashed whatever was breakable. And they found not one dangerous implement or document. They could have done one thing: placed guns and swords in the very ditches they had dug and then said I had hidden them. But this they were unable to do because the mutessarif, knowing they would attempt it, had sent his personal police to keep an eye open for any such trickery.

My God! Why does a Turkish official show such solicitude for a giavoor? I have done no favor to him. Why does he not send off this giavoor too with other thousands to perish? Why, at the risk of his own life, does he protect and preserve me?

"I have commanded him to do thus, and he is constrained. I shall protect you in all ways. I shall protect, but not deliver you from temptations, but lead you through terrible trials, that you may understand me well and become a living witness of my Power and Salvation."

Tired by their search, and disappointed, the mob left my church. Unsatisfied, they sent a gendarme to the pasha, asking permission to search my house, but the pasha sent a definite refusal. My enemies went away. And I, alone, entered God's sanctuary and once again glorified him.

It was on this day that about a hundred young men of rich Armenian families, soldiers in the Turkish Army serving out their terms, were suddenly arrested (no cause being given), disarmed, and driven out of the city to an unknown place, leaving their families in deep mourning.

On April 20, Holy Thursday, one of the days of Christ's passion, the agony of the Armenians was repeated. Gendarmes, holding in their hands the list of the families to be deported—families of the wealthy class, many of them belonging to the Catholic community—swarmed through the Armenian quarters and drove the dwellers out with their whips. There was no sparing the old, the children, the women. There was no mercy shown those venerable persons in whose presence they had previously stood with folded hands and spoken respectfully. Pushing, kicking, cursing were the lot of those same Armenian aghas around whose tables many times the Turkish officials had gathered, eaten, drunk, spoken flatteringly, and from whom they had borrowed thousands of gold pieces. Today, by orders of these officials, their former hosts were being whipped out of their houses. Leaving behind their palatial mansions, fertile fields, fruitful gardens, vineyards, and fabulous riches, they passed through the city streets with only the clothes on their backs. They were taken far away from the city—a large group, nearly a thousand people —and driven toward the graveyard of their former countrymen, like them to suffer torture and to die.

On Sunday, April 30, my kind pasha called to him one of the members of my church board, a personal friend of his, and told him to notify me that the time had come when it was no longer possible for him to protect me; that the *Ittihat* had threatened him and would surely deport me with all the members of my family. At the first opportunity I should flee from the city, at which time he would do all in his power to keep my wife and children from deportation.

My friend found it extremely difficult to give me this ill news personally. He therefore revealed it to another member of

73

the board, requesting him to assume this heavy office. A friend's compassion thus feels another's grief.

This was a most bitter situation! To leave my wife, my children, the remnant of my flock, my work, my obligations! Where could I leave my loved ones? True, the pasha promised, but he too was in a precarious position and probably would soon be removed. And again, where was I to go? How was it possible for me to escape? Every place was full of soldiers and murderous Turks, and the order had been given openly that wherever an Armenian was seen alone any Turk had the right to kill him.

I knelt down in my room and spoke to my Heavenly Father, requesting his help. Then I called my wife and told her, and together we knelt and prayed. After our prayer, the first thought that came to me was to appeal to the German missionaries and ask their opinion as to what I should do. I found perfect concern in these friends, who recommended that I go to Baghtche, a city two days' journey from Marash, where German officials were busy in the construction of the Berlin-Baghdad Railroad. I could work there as a laborer under German protection. In a few days one of these German officials would come to Marash and they would try to send me back with him. Upon my burning heart this news was like a cooling drop of water.

I continued my church and civic duties as before, telling my people nothing about my leaving. On May 3 another convoy of Armenians was deported, and I always bore in my heart the fear that *Ittihat* would not give me an opportunity to withdraw from the city but, suddenly mingling me with the deportees, send me away too. On Friday, May 5, the German official, Mr. Klaus, came to Marash and went on toward Albustan. My German friends spoke with him and arranged for my departure. I hired a muleteer and packing my absolute necessities in a bundle and a box sent them to Baghtche. I made arrangements with the American missionaries for the church work to be carried out and appointed the aged pastor, Rev. Kevork Kazarjian, in my stead.

It was Sunday, May 7. Although the congregation was unaware of the situation, I knew this was my last time with them.

During the morning service I spoke on Isaiah 26:20-21 and in the evening on Matthew 26:38-39. The former verses gave us the message "Come, my people, enter thou into thy chambers, and shut thy doors about thee: hide thyself as it were for a little moment, until the indignation be overpast. For, behold, the Lord cometh out of his place to punish the inhabitants of the earth for their iniquity: the earth also shall disclose her blood, and shall no more cover her slain." The latter verses read, "Then saith he unto them, My soul is exceeding sorrowful, even unto death: tarry ye here, and watch with me. And he went a little farther, and fell on his face, and prayed, saying, O my Father, if it be possible, let this cup pass from me: nevertheless, not as I will, but as thou wilt." At the end of the service we sang the 194th hymn from the Turkish hymnal: "*Gideceğim*. I must go. I cannot see my way. But it is sufficient that the Lord knows where I go." And silently, with a broken heart, I gave my farewell to my flock.

On May 8, 9, and 10 I arranged my household and church work as well as I could. I led the week's prayer meeting and the women's prayer meeting. Then I was ready to depart.

But on Wednesday, May 10, some military officers came and investigated the school building, a number of whose rooms I had occupied with my family. Since the whole building was to be used by the soldiers, we must vacate these rooms immediately and move somewhere else. My plans had been to leave my wife and children here, but now I realized how foolish that would have been. If they had remained, surrounded on all sides by Turkish families, what could not have happened to them, especially in the darkness and loneliness of night! Besides, here, always in the public eye, how easily and soon they would have been discovered by the Turkish officials! How natural would have been their deportation at any time! Yet if I had asked the missionaries to receive my family into their circles, I was certain they would have refused, objecting, "Their present dwelling is adequate." Now that I was forced to leave this building, I had a strong reason to expect them to take in my family. As events will show, if my loved ones had remained where they were, they would all have been lost.

The American missionaries gave my family a place, and on May 11 we moved. Here they were comparatively safe, and far from the sight of the Turks. I passed my last night with them.

On Friday morning, May 12, I arose very early. I prayed. I kissed my wife and beloved children. My eldest son was twelve years old, my eldest daughter eight, my second daughter six, my third daughter four, and my little boy was one, still nursing. I said goodby to them and to my friends in the building. Leaving behind my city, my flock, my unhappy remnant, in a flood of tears and with a melting heart I set forth with Mr. Klaus, who had returned from Albustan, for Baghtche. We traveled the whole day and the first three hours of night. When we reached our destination, fortunately I found one of my former friends. I supped with him, and that night I slept on alien soil.

7

On the railroad line about one hour's journey from Baghtche thousands of workers were laboring. Among them were twelve thousand or so Armenian men, women, and children, gathered from here and there by German officers, to be used, at a loaf of bread a day, to complete the line. Although they were slaves subjected to dire deprivation and exhausting toil, still they were content with their condition, believing that they had escaped the sword, the bullet, and the cursed tortures of deportation. They at least had the privilege of dying a natural death under racking labors and extreme poverty.

I had come to share their fate. I placed my box and bundle with the belongings of a number of friends and, together with them, entered an old, stinking, filthy tent, to be a tent dweller. Sufferings of every kind were to be my lot. But I was comforted that my loved ones were safe in Marash, and that I too was safe, and earning my daily bread.

May 14 was the first Sunday of my deportation. Friends came together. We prayed. We consoled each other. And the day passed in that way.

On Monday Mr. Klaus assigned me the office of miller. He introduced me to seven helpers and three donkeys and sent us to a mill about an hour's distance from the station, to grind grain and produce flour. *"Usta iken olduk şakirt. Al bardaği yek su getir!* A craftsman, I became an apprentice. Take the jug and bring some water!" I left the ministry and became a miller. I used to lead men. Now I began to lead donkeys. But I was content with this also, for the night was to be darker yet.

I had had no experience as a miller, and with the exception of one of my helpers the rest knew nothing about the trade either. Like me, they belonged to the professional class. They were college graduates, teachers, professors, before this slavery fell upon them. Nevertheless, we devoted ourselves to our work.

The water ran. The millstone turned. The grain was poured out. The flour was ground. We bagged the flour, loaded the bags on the donkeys, and, taking them to the station, stored them in a granary. During the first hours of the morning we did well. Presently, however, we discovered that, although on one side the flour was being ground, on the other side the grain was running out continuously and swimming away on the stream, wasted. The wooden axle of the bottom millstone, we found, had a hole in it, and the wheat was escaping through that. Here was great loss. But what was worse, the company considered the workers responsible for any damage, and we whose wages were a loaf of bread a day, how were we to pay! In deep anxiety, we could only continue to work. Thus, turning a part of the wheat into flour and offering the rest as a sacrifice to the stream, we passed the whole day. But when night came on, the work apportioned for that day had not yet been completed. We therefore continued, hungry and tired, until it was finished. We put some of the flour in the bags we had, leaving most of it in the mill, and with the companionship and under the guidance of the donkeys, we returned to the station, sent the donkeys to their stable, and entered ours.

In the morning, with the same friends, and with the same solemnity, we went to our working place. But what should we see? The mill had been broken into during the night and all the flour stolen. I ran back to the station and informed Mr. Klaus of the theft. He was very kind in his dealing with me and himself undertook the capture of the thieves. Then I returned to my work.

The first thing we had to do was repair the mill. I granted

our three donkey friends a long intermission, and we seven bipeds set to work. After a few hours everything was fixed and the millstone turned again. The flour was being ground. The donkeys resumed their labors.

The gentleman who knew something about this trade directed us, and I began to learn its ins and outs, convinced that for some time to come I was to remain in this new office.

On Wednesday I headed toward the stable, to call on my donkey friends, to learn their well-being, and to request them, if they were willing, to join me and go to our working place. But alas! They were not there!

"Where are the donkeys?" I said to the keeper.

Pointing lazily far out into the plain, he answered, "There. Someone came, and with his own donkeys drove yours along too."

This was a sad situation. Without the donkeys we would be unable to work and so be deprived of our loaf of bread! Suddenly I began to run toward the donkeys, shouting, "*Ei-hoo! Ei-hoo!*" I was perspiring, panting, my mouth and lips were dry, but I kept on running. When the thief saw that I was gaining on him, he drove the donkeys faster. At last I caught up and stopped him and a heated quarrel began. I was happy that the donkeys declared neutrality and that I was matched with only one ass. Although my opponent was a gigantic and powerful Turk, I discovered that I could shout much louder than he. Finally my voice prevailed over his body and I became the victor. I separated my three donkeys. But because my enemy had been defeated it was necessary that he pay an additional indemnity. I saw that three of the remaining donkeys belonged to a man who was operating another mill near ours. He too would be left idle if he did not have his animals. So wishing to help him, I demanded them also and received them. Thus the battle ended with my triumph. The defeated Turk went away with his own donkeys.

Now I had six donkeys to drive to the working places. I had never in my life learned the art of driving donkeys and would have thought it very simple. But if you ever try it, you will discover that it is not such an easy art.

The donkeys had saddles on their backs, but their necks were free. They had no halters. There were ropes on both sides of the saddles, to fasten the burdens. I had seen muleteers with long sticks in their hands, but I had no such instrument. Nevertheless, surely out of respect for a pastor my three donkey friends would walk on obediently and the other three would follow. I was greatly disappointed. All the donkeys had signed a secret agreement and had decided to rebel.

I shouted *Cho! Cho!* I tried to persuade them to walk. They would not budge. With my hand I struck the head of this one, the back of that one, another's tail. But who cared? They had made a pact! At no price would they obey me. If they moved, they never went in the direction I desired, but always away from me—and away from each other.

Was I so small that I could not make these donkeys understand sense? My self-respect was wounded. I had to do something! These donkeys had to obey. Oh, I would tie the donkeys behind each other with the ropes of their saddles and pull the foremost one along, while all the rest followed. But with whatever strength and in whatever direction I pulled, the rebels pulled with sixfold strength in opposite and different directions. Now I became stubborn and would not cease my attempt. When the donkeys understood that there was sufficient strength on my side and an equally long-eared stubbornness, after a momentary deliberation they adopted a new plan. They would blow up the bridge!

Suddenly the saddle of one of them slid off his back and hung beneath his belly. A second followed. And then a third. Then all the rest! And with great dexterity they turned around each other and got completely entangled in the ropes. Everything became tied to everything else. On the plain was a mess of donkeys, an immovable pyramid.

Although the donkeys were panting under the weight of the saddles hanging from their bellies, and were suffering because of the tight ropes gripping them, they seemed very content because they had defeated me. I could do nothing but accept my defeat.

Bewildered and starting to sob, I raised my hands to heaven. "O my Father, as far as I know I was ordained to be the pastor of men. Now, contrary to the purpose of that ordination, here I have been ordained the pastor of donkeys. No matter what, I am willing to perform this office too. But I have not been trained for it. You should have taught me first and then ordained me. Help me, I beg. Now one of these poor donkeys will burst or else I will go mad. Send some help."

And there in the distance someone was coming toward me! I was glad that, although a stranger, he was a co-suffering Armenian. He saw my condition. He pitied. I asked his aid. He untied the ropes, straightened the saddles, lined up the donkeys before him, and with the blows of his stick drove them to our working place. I returned the three donkeys to my friend. It was then about noon, and for that day we earned a half-day's wages.

On Saturday we had finished our work and were about to rest a little when we were startled by a threatening bray. One of our donkeys, unable to control his revengeful spirit, stiffened his tail and ran off. He had a value of ten liras. If he got lost, what would we do? We had to catch him, for ten liras were not to be found among us seven bipeds. One of us remaining at the mill, the rest ran after the fugitive. But we soon lost his trail. For hours we wandered in the night before giving up to spend a little time in anxious sleep.

In the morning, half asleep, half awake, we quickly scattered again and finally found the rebellious donkey and brought him back. He promised not to make such a great mistake again.

It was Sunday, May 21. We were not working. In the afternoon we wanted to take a walk and so set out to a place about an hour's journey from our tent, a place called *Ayran Poonaru*. We expected to see a number of friends, to be comforted by their presence. But suddenly a gendarme stopped us and led us to his *ellibaşï*, his superior officer. The *ellibaşï* was from Marash, a good man, and one who knew me. He said kindly, "If it had been someone else in my place, he would have immediately arrested you and sent you to the prison of Baghtche to be deported from there. This is the order for all Armenians going from one center to another. But I shall take pity on you. I will not arrest you. Quickly go back where you came from and busy yourselves with your work."

I thanked him. We all bowed before him and returned to our tent. We had forgotten that we were captive slaves in chains.

On Monday evening, May 22, a young man appeared at our tent. Who was he? A Zeytoontsi!

Cholakian Aram Bey and his Braves, after escaping from the battle of Fundejak, had taken refuge on a mountain near us called Giavoor Dagh. There, with a number of Fundejaktsis and other Braves, they were holding their own. Sometimes they attacked the Turkish villages near by, in order to get provisions; often the Turkish villagers, to be free from their attacks, would supply them willingly. The government knew about this. How many times troops had been sent against them! The Braves remained there till the very end of the war, then went to Aleppo and were received with glory and honor by the English.

This young man was one of them. He had dared to descend the mountain and reach us. When we learned who he was, we fell into great fear. If in any way it was discovered that he had come to us, eaten bread with us, spoken with us—oh, that was enough for our destruction! We were certainly able to seize him, tie him up, and hand him over to the government. But how could we have betrayed an Armenian, our own blood-kin, to the Turks! We gave him bread and he ate. This was a most unforgivable crime! We pleaded with him to go away quickly, but he insisted on remaining with us the whole night. In the morning, before dawn, he departed.

On Tuesday evening he returned. As long as he was with us, we trembled and had no rest or sleep. About midnight four strangers passed by. We all got to our feet and lit a light. "Who are you? What do you want?" we shouted. This was not the thunderous voice of bravery but the fear of timid men.

The strangers did not answer us. But as they disappeared, they threw stones at us. Who were they? Why had they come? We never found out. All night we had no sleep. Near morning the Zeytoontsi again departed and we never saw him after that.

We kept this matter entirely secret and continued our work through that week. On May 28, Sunday, the German officials decided to stop the work at the mill. Thus my career as a miller came to an end after two weeks.

My friends began to work as laborers, like thousands of other Armenians, with spade and pickax. I was favored with the position of supervisor over the warehouses. Among twelve thousand Armenians, I was perhaps the most fortunate, working in a building, in the shade, comfortably. All the rest were beneath the scorching sun, digging the hard earth and breaking rocks. Even women and children carried stones and soil on their backs. All were in rags, barefooted, filthy, worn out, skeleton-thin. And after unbearable labors, they used to enter old, stinking, lousy tents at night and chew on dry dark bread, then lie down on the bare ground to sleep. How many rich men and delicate women belonging to notable and influential families were here, partaking of these hardships with the rest! It broke my heart to see frail girls of my nation stumbling under loads which bowed them almost to the earth! But they were comforted by the thought that here they were somewhat protected.

The days passed. On Sunday, June 4, a number of us went to an Armenian village near by, one that had not yet felt the curse of deportation since—thanks to the German officials!—laborers were required to work on the railroad line. Here a good woman, seeing our filthy condition, took pity on us. She heated water and we washed ourselves and felt somewhat refreshed.

On Wednesday, June 7, letters came from Marash. All the Armenian people of Marash, I among them, felt consternation and dread. It was written: "The order for the deportation of the remaining Armenians has been given, and group on group, they are being driven away. Not one Armenian will be left."

What could we do for our loved ones? We wept. We prayed. I appealed to Mr. Klaus and informed him of the situation. He advised us to try, if it were possible, to bring our families to Baghtche. He gave us permits and sent his servant to Marash with a message to the pasha, asking him to let our families go. I too wrote a letter, to my family. The servant set out on Friday, June 9. I felt safe about myself and about this place and was looking forward to having my family with me in safety. I had fallen into the sea; I was grasping at the waves.

The servant had reached Marash and I was anxiously awaiting the arrival of my loved ones. But *eyvah parasïz ansavori!* Alas, to the glory that was! I was passing my time in dreams and illusions, not knowing that the danger threatening Marash was also threatening us. Soon all these wretched laborers, uprooted how many times, would again be forced to walk the hellish road!

On Tuesday, June 13, the military pasha of Adana came to Baghtche. He had recently been at Van, trying to exterminate the Armenians there, but had been defeated and dishonored. Consequently he was a monster of vengefulness and everlasting hatred of Armenians. With his bloodthirsty soldiers and gendarmes he surrounded the unhappy people.

We were caught in a military chain, and all of us were going to be deported. Hopelessness! Abandonment! Bitter sorrow! Black hell! Who shall I think of? Myself? My loved ones? I to be sent off in one direction, my family in another, far, far away from each other! Alone! Alone! To be tortured, despised, torn piecemeal, annihilated! *Asdvadz im!* Oh, my God!

By Wednesday, June 14, the Eintilli deportation had begun—second in horribleness only to the Der-el-Zor deportation, because Der-el-Zor always remains the first. Group after group was brought to Baghtche. Three days had been set aside to herd them in one concentration camp. Wretched Armenians! Again beneath the cutting whips, under the heavy blows of butts of guns, they were leaving their tents, their few possessions, and holding their children's hands were running toward the slaughterhouse.

I was still in my tent. Mr. Klaus was trying to save me, telling the Turkish officers that I was a religious man, and not one who would meddle in politics. But "Badveli is just the man we want," they said. "He knows how to speak. He is educated. He can lead the people. Those who harm us most are these leaders, and we intend to get rid of them."

On Friday morning, June 16, Mr. Klaus's servant returned from Marash. There was a letter for me from my wife. It had been impossible to get permission to leave Marash. In my woe I was somewhat comforted by this news, for if my family had set out, they too would have been on the road with me. And I could not have borne that!

84

1914-1918

I am in the furnace of Nebuchadnezzar, but Divine Presence is with me; He views every seemingly insignificant particular and leads me step by step; wheresoever He sends me He will go with me.

Mr. Klaus, with heavy heart, revealed to me the fruitlessness of his efforts to save my life. In a little while I too would be taken to the concentration camp.

For the last time I entered my tent. I took my umbrella, some clothes in a bag, some bread, a water jug, and a thin quilt. I left my cot and a number of cooking utensils and tools. I put my Bible in my bag too and, after saying a prayer, was ready for the slaughterers to come and take me. A monster-like *zaptiye* appeared before me and said, "Are you papaz Abraham?"

"Yes," I answered.

"Walk!" he commanded.

I obeyed. I had begun the road of death, the road of horror. Tears rolled down my cheeks, but my lips were softly murmuring, "Though my God slay me, yet will I trust in him." As I advanced I saw many gendarmes, searching every corner to drive out hiding Armenians. One of these snatched my umbrella from my hand. The Armenian had lost every right! Everything now belonged to the Turk. This was the first step of deportation, and I was walking under the scorching sun. But at least I was a man. What were the mothers to do? Mothers who had been deported from other places already! Mothers who had lost their husbands and sons! Mothers who had small ones with them! Should they bewail the loss of their loved ones? Their darlings were hungry and thirsty. Should they think of their need? They were unable to walk. How could they bear their children on their shoulders and arms? My good God! Thou shouldst not have allowed it!

I soon reached the concentration camp, where twelve thousand Armenians had been herded—hungry, thirsty, naked, dirty, exhausted, already near death.

It is fear and trembling that prevail everywhere. Gendarmes, like bloodthirsty wolves, circle the convoy unceasingly.

85

Neither To Laugh nor To Weep

Whose burden shall I bear? Mine? My loved ones'? My nation's? What shall the girls and widows do—women who have already lost their fathers, husbands, brothers? And now to sate the lust of Turkish beasts and then to be mercilessly killed! Many of these women are cutting their hair, smearing mud on their faces in order to appear ugly and detestable and thus evade the lustful eye of the Turk.

This day the first convoy was put on its way—a convoy composed of young men, the Braves, more than one thousand, all separated from their wives, children, parents. Lashed forward, they had no opportunity to weep. But those who watched them go, who knew that this was the last separation, were beating their breasts and clawing the earth and screaming convulsively.

Suddenly a *yuzbaşï* called me by name. I thought I too was going to be put into this first convoy. To tell the truth, I was happy. No matter what my end was, I wanted to approach it quickly.

But instead of leading me toward the convoy, he took me in another direction, to a stable, and ordered me to go in. About twenty other Armenians were there—teachers, professors, ministers. Now I too was imprisoned with them and the stable door was closed.

Why had they brought us here, separating us from the rest? We were the leaders of our people—such great criminals that we were not worthy to be deported but would be dispatched another way. We were to be raised on the gallows, in the presence of the Turkish mob, for their joy, and for the consternation of the deportees.

The stable also housed the *binbaşï's* horse. The floor was covered with manure. The ceiling was veiled with a moldy dirtiness. The air was extremely foul. There was no water to drink. The thought that perhaps our families too had set out on the road was torturing us. We ourselves were already in the jaws of death; but when, through the cracks in the door, we saw our beloved countrymen betrayed to dishonor and slow death, there was no life left in us.

I took my Bible and in the dim light read some verses of promise. Walking back and forth, I prayed silently, beseeching power from above; and sometimes, exhausted, I sat down on the manure.

A gendarme came to water the *binbaşi*'s horse. We begged him to give us a drink. In return for some money, he gave us about a pitcherful, and drop by drop we sipped it in turn, as if it were the cup of the Lord's communion.

Darkness fell. The stable was now a dungeon. We talked to each other in whispers. At the same time what things were going on outside!

We hear the children's screams, the mothers' sobs. They are hungry, they are thirsty, and they are cold in the night air. They have no place to rest. They cannot freely move their bowels. They are suffering. They are visualizing the unbearable journey of the next day and its horrors, and they are going mad. The young girls and prettier women are being snatched away, and zaptiye *satisfy their lust on them. There are secret murders. And some, unable to bear these things, drop dead.*

It was midnight. There was a terrifying shriek. We were all immediately on our feet, trembling. What had happened? A scorpion had fallen from the ceiling and stung someone. He was poisoned and writhing in pain. What could we do? Nothing.

There is no light. We cannot see each other. We hear the groaning of our friend. We turn here and there blindly. We are afraid to sit down. Perhaps the scorpion will sting us too. With open eyes we see horrible nothings and bump into each other. Our hands are always on our heads and necks. In truth I have suffered hell!

A little later a gendarme came, holding a lamp in his hand, to count us. We told him of our condition. He placed a guard there and left the door open. Now at least we could breathe a little fresh air. I went to the door and had the temerity to ask the guard if I might stretch out a little while before the door and rest. Receiving permission, I lay down on my side. And suddenly my eyes filled with tears. I remembered my home, my soft bed. Now I was stretched out on a rock. Here sleep drowned me. But soon the rays of the sun fell on my eyes and I withdrew into my dungeon.

It was Saturday, June 17. The work of deportation continued the whole day, before our eyes, and we, from moment to moment, were awaiting hanging and an end to this unbearable life. We passed the night as before, except that the scorpion did not sting us again. It seems that she at first was unaware of the insufferable existence of the Armenian people, but when she learned the truth, she was ashamed of what she had done. She pitied us and withdrew, not wishing to repeat her sting. The scorpion was kinder than the Turk.

The next day the number of deportees had decreased. Many had been sent and the rest were going. We continued to wait in the same hopeless condition.

A little before sunset a policeman came into the stable and ordered us to go out and line up before the door. Were we to be taken and hanged now? After a while the *kaymakam* of Baghtche and the military pasha appeared before us. The latter began to cross-examine us one by one: "Who are you? Where do you come from? Why did you come here? Do you have a wife and children? Where are they?"

After we had all been catechized, he grimaced at us and said, "We're going to deport you all from here and your families from their places. This is why we wanted your names and addresses." I was overcome with dismay. My wife, my angels, my innocent and holy children! to be given over to the hands of these beasts! For an eternal moment I closed my eyes, and with an inner and voiceless aim I shot toward heaven a wordless supplication. "*Asdvadz im!* Oh, my God! Pour out all thy punishments, thy wrath, thy fire on me! Let thy arrows pierce my side and my heart! Gladly will I endure and willingly! But spare my wife, my children!" This experience was a perfect revelation to me. At that moment I understood clearly the significance of Christ's death and vicarious sacrifice, and the remission, forgiveness, and redemption established by it.

Our inquisition ended, we were back in the stable. At least

the fear of being hanged was no more. I stretched out on the manure and slept. Toward morning the *zaptiye* came and took away all but me and two others. Were those who went fortunate or those who remained? Who could tell? An hour later another *zaptiye* came and took us three also and shoved us among the deportees.

The last convoy of about fifteen hundred was being prepared to be put on the road. Beginning with the strongest and bravest, the Armenians of these parts had been sent away, and only this weakest group was left. In rounding up each company there was no consideration of family, kinship, or friendship ties. The husband was torn from his wife, the son from his mother, the bride from her groom. Where were my friends? Who knows? Who knows what befell the Armenians sent before us? Our convoy was made up mostly of widows, old folks, the weak, children, left-overs! No one family had been left entire.

As I waited for the group to move, I saw an angel-like child, about two years old, sleeping the sweet sleep of morn on a piece of straw matting. Suddenly she awoke. She looked around. Everything was strange. There was no mother to caress her. She began a heartrending wail. I wept. Oh, this sting was more venomous than that of the scorpion or the snake! That child was left there. Many other small children were left there.

A little farther off I saw a young *zaptiye* walk up to an Armenian girl about eighteen years old, delicate and beautiful. He held her by the arm and began to speak to her. The girl shook her head. Peeved, the *zaptiye* shoved her back into the group and went away. When I asked the girl what the man had said, she answered, "He wants me to become a Moslem and marry him. I refused. I will not become the wife of a Turk."

I learned that this girl was a native of Adapazar, a graduate of the Armenian girls' school there, well educated, morally upright, and the daughter of a wealthy and refined family. Her whole family had been deported. Having lost her father, mother, sisters, and brothers, she was the only survivor. Though driven from place to place and suffering constantly, she had preserved her faith and her honor and was enduring uncomplainingly.

I looked in another direction: An aged father, a young

mother, two small children were shedding tears over a corpse stretched out on the ground. It was the aged father's son, the young mother's husband, the small children's beloved father. Not able to bear the tortures which had been inflicted upon him, that night he had died. His loved ones were giving their last farewell to him. They left him and joined the rest of us.

Under the guard of about fifty wolfish, merciless, savage *zaptiye*, the convoy moved. This was the first time in my life that I was traveling on foot, a burden on my back. But I was perhaps the most fortunate man in this group. I was strong, still young. I did not have the care of wife and children, at least for the present. I had only myself to carry along. What could the mothers do? Mothers with one, two, three children! I saw mothers with bags on their backs full of dry bread, a child at the breast, holding the hand of another child, walking along. Slowly? Resting now and then? Ah, that would have been well. But it was not so. They had to walk unceasingly and fast because the whip was ready at any moment to slash whatever part of their body it met.

Those who became exhausted and fell were left where they dropped. No one was allowed to stop and help them. Either they remained there to be tortured for days by hunger, thirst, cold, and heat, and then died, or else, if they were fortunate, they were killed immediately by the bullet or the dagger of a *zapitye* or a passing *başïbozuk*.

Walking continuously thus, panting, exhausted, leaving many on the way, we reached the foot of a mountain, and the convoy in one body fell on the ground breathless. Soon the *zaptiye* dismounted and ordered the men and women to gather in separate places. We knew what this signified. The *zaptiye* went among the women and girls, separated the prettier ones, and before our very eyes raped them cruelly until morning, even the small girls, many of whom died under the terror and agony.

At night a north wind began to blow. Soaked with sweat from the day's heat and exhaustion, we began to shiver. My teeth chattered. My whole body quaked. And think in what condition the women and children were! I asked a young man near me whom I recognized from Marash to press his back to mine and warm me. This helped us both.

Early in the morning Tuesday, June 20, we were on our way again. After we had traveled only two hours, the order was given: "Everyone line up, four abreast!"

We lined up, to be driven over the mountain, between huge rocks, through muddy and inextricable paths, without turning right or left, a group of fifteen hundred souls!

We must walk. And we must walk quickly, quickly! Under the lashes of whips, beaten with the butts of rifles! We are walking. We are running! Panting! Gasping! We are running away from the lashing and the beating! But what should the old people do? The women? The weak? The children? The mothers holding their babes? They stumble, roll, are tramped under foot.

Hundreds were falling. The fallen were being shot or were left to their fate. And the convoy, without resting, its breath broken, its mouth burned, was walking and walking.

Some time later the horrid scene of hell was revealed before us! Corpses! Corpses! Murdered! Mutilated! Corpses of Armenian men, women, and children! Stepping over them like ghosts of the dead, we walked and walked. There was no need of taking us to Der-el-Zor and massacring us there! Armenians were being massacred on the way between Baghtche and Marash. To see the scene of Der-el-Zor, it was not necessary to go to the desert! The perfect counterpart was here. Here were the bodies of those driven out before us and shot, stabbed, savagely slaughtered! I had heard what deportation was. I had imagined it. Now I saw it with my own eyes. Our convoy, despite all its sufferings, was the most fortunate. The previous convoys had experienced more!

The men in our group who struck the eyes of the *zaptiye* were separated, taken a little distance away, and shot. Everyone expected his turn to come next. The old man whose young son had died in Baghtche was walking along beside me with his daughter-in-law and two small grandchildren. His breath was consumed. The fainting widow was helping her children with one hand and supporting her father-in-law with the other. But now, unable to walk, he was getting in the way of those behind. A *zaptiye* saw him. He came and kicked him and, dragging him out of the group, tripped him into a ditch near by and emptied his gun into his breast. The widow, horrified, drew back, and kept on going with her two children.

About this time one of the *zaptiye* came up to me. He placed his Mauser on my breast. I thought my last moment had come. But he did not empty his gun. Looking at me he said, *"Seni öldüreyim mi?* Shall I kill you?"* Why? Why does he ask me? Why does he not shoot and stretch me out on the ground too?

I answered him humbly, "You know, friend. If you have mercy on me, you will not kill me; but if you wish, I am in your hands, you can kill."

He lowered his gun and went away, most certainly to shoot other Armenians.

Thus, the exhausted fell, not to rise again. Those who could keep on their feet walked under the burning sun—tired, hungry, thirsty, benumbed by horror, with death grinning at their side.

I had a leathern water bottle containing about a cupful of water. The children near me were crying, *"Choor! Choor!* Water! Water!"* Hastily, lest I be seen by a *zaptiye*, I held out the bottle here and there and wet the children's lips with a few drops. I think those drops were very precious, and that they were recorded in the book of heaven.

It was afternoon, and the convoy reached a field near Fundejak, where we were allowed to rest a little. In complete exhaustion, I fell on the ground and began to sleep as did the others. But soon, the leader of the *zaptiye* rounded up a number of the men he thought rich and ordered, "Get together three hundred liras and hand them over; if not, I'll take all of you and any other men I choose to the mountains and massacre you."

This was reported to the convoy. A new woe! Everyone brought forth whatever he had, and, robbed in this way, we passed the danger of slaughter.

A little later we were again put on our way, and after traveling two more hours, we stopped for the night on the bank of a small stream. This last two hours' walk was comparatively comfortable. But the reason was not that a little pity had been born in the *zaptiye;* it was only that they were tired of their murders and beatings, and their leader was busy dividing the three hundred liras which he had taken from us.

An Armenian priest was sitting next to me. He had been deported again and again and now once more was on the road. He had borne the same burdens as I, had seen the same scenes. Like me and even more, in the depths of his heart his flock's terrible slavery and deportation had left unhealing wounds. Furthermore, his wife and several of his children had fallen by the roadside. His two sons were with him.

The clear water of the stream was flowing resplendent. But on the other bank, from among rocks, a fountain was gushing forth, more clear, more pure. We were all drinking from the stream. Our priest father called one of his sons to him. Giving him his drinking flask, he told the boy to ford the stream and fill the flask from the fountain and bring him to drink.

I said to him, *"Der Hayr,* lord father, the water of this stream is enough for us. After this day we shall be in places where the dirtiest and most putrid waters will taste refreshing."

Der Hayr answered, "Not so, friend. Even in our most hopeless condition we must be brave. As men, our duty is always to do our best, to live life as well as possible. Now, since we can drink a clearer and a purer water, let us drink it. And when we come to bad waters, let us try to choose the best among the bad and drink that."

Der Hayr was right. He drank the water of the fountain and gave me to drink of it. And this new moral strength issuing from one of our Armenian prophets inspired me with new life. Why does not the Armenian nation die? The flaming bush burns but is not consumed. I marveled that even in this hellish condition the deportees were still talking with each other, encouraging each other, even smiling and laughing. The Armenian is the prophecy of the world!

Hardly had we rested when the Moslem hordes from the surrounding villages—with guns, axes, animals, sacks—gathered near the convoy. They had come to kill us and carry off our clothes and whatever else they could get. This is exactly what they had done to the convoys before us. Why, these poor fools, they were being blessed by Allah! For successively the Almighty was sending them thousands of unarmed giavoors with real clothes on their backs and money and shoes! All they had to do was swoop down from the mountains, slay these helpless ones, and reap the bounteous harvest—a reward for their religious fervor!

But this time they were disappointed. The head of the *zaptiye* did not allow them to massacre us. No, this convoy still had gold and women.

Night fell, and again the defilements belonging to darkness began. The prettier women were taken aside and raped. Among them was an extremely beautiful girl, about twenty-five years of age. During the day the *zaptiye* had disputed over her: "I'm going to have her!" "No, by Allah, I'm going to have her!" At night, one after the other, they raped that holy virgin, and then, killing her, threw her mutilated corpse to one side because they could not agree who should have her.

The deed of the afternoon was repeated. "Collect five hundred liras and hand them over; if not, all of you will be massacred!" One by one every individual searched himself, and whatever was left was handed over. Then we rested a few hours, wet under the dew of the open air, on the uneven ground.

With the rising sun we too arose. It was Wednesday, June 21. I saw an old man who had been in the convoy before us. He had not been able to go on and had been left there. This morning he set out with us, but he could hardly walk. A *zaptiye* ordered him to go on, and the old man, hauling himself about, advanced a few steps. Then the *zaptiye* emptied his gun in his back and spread him out on the ground. I think that that old man was fortunate.

Then we saw the bloody, naked corpse of that twenty-five-year-old girl who had been used cruelly all the previous night. Beside a young man, shot but still alive, from the convoy before us sat his wife, comforting him. There was nothing else she could have done for him. One of the *zaptiye* grabbed the wife by the hand and drove her into our group, then emptied his gun in the young man's breast and shut his half-open eyes. Certainly if that man could have spoken, he would have thanked the executioner who had ended his torture.

We were now nearing our stopping place, about two hours' journey from Marash, and the *zaptiye* had to make their last gleaning. They scattered among the convoy and took whatever they could take—a hat, a shoe, a gown, a belt, a watch. Shooting, beating, pushing, shoving! They took and they took!

Ahead of us was a cucumber garden. Those who had a few *metelikler* left bought some cucumbers and began to eat them ravenously. I wanted a cucumber too but I did not have the money to buy one. I began to sob like a child.

Still on! We reached a stream called Ak Soo. The water was deep. A few weeks previously I had crossed this stream on horseback. Now I was about to wade to the other side. How were the women and children going to cross? Whose concern? In this or that way, and always in torture, the Armenian people were to be exterminated.

Taking off our shoes and rolling up our clothes, we poured into the current. I do not know how many children were drowned. But their mothers were happy that their children were dying an easy death. The thought of suicide, with the swiftness of lightning, came and vanished from my mind. "Let yourself go in the water and all will be silence." Why do men commit suicide? What is their mental condition previous to their act? I now understand. "When thou passest through the waters, I will be with thee; and through the rivers, they shall not overflow thee" (Isaiah 43:2).

I was across, on the dry bank. But for many the stream became their grave.

After walking another hour, we reached our stopping place. Again we stretched out on the ground and tried to rest.

When the remnants of the convoys sent ahead of us stopped here, their relatives from Marash were not permitted to come to see them. After being kept here awhile, they were driven to strange places, and perhaps by now all of them were dead. Now I understood how my imprisonment in the stable for three days had saved me from the more terrible evils borne by the previous convoys.

As we rested, some Armenian women from Marash came to look for their loved ones. Those who found them burst into tears as they embraced. Others shed tears alone. And the rest of us wept too, but the falling drops were washing away the bitterness in our hearts.

The sharp gaze of one of the women fell upon me. She was a member of my church. Suddenly she ran toward me and put her arms around me. "Badveli, we thought you were dead. We mourned for you. Your wife and children are still in mourning. But praise God you are alive!"

Now I had two streams of happiness: my family had not been deported and I was alive. I said to this woman, "Mary, quickly return to the city, and like Magdalene of old, tell everyone that I have risen from the dead!"

Quickly I wrote a few lines to my wife and gave the note to Mary. And near nightfall I saw my son Albert, then twelve years of age, coming to see his deported father. As I recall that scene my heart bleeds. I ran and greeted him. I embraced him, both of us weeping. I asked about the others and learned that the order for their deportation had been given and that Mother was preparing everything to set out on the journey!

Alas! My poor wife! She does not know what deportation is! She thinks that she and the children, sitting in carriages, with food, water, clothes, coverings, traveling comfortably and safely, will go to a nearby city to stay a few months and then return! "Mother is making the preparations." Alas! Simplehearted and sincere holy one! All these things are for only one or two hours. Then everything will be taken away. Your animals will be seized. You, your babe in your arms, and trying to keep track of the other children, will walk. In a little while the children will begin to cry with fatigue, thirst, hunger. You too will grow weak. You will be forced to leave your little ones as they cry, "Mother, don't leave us here!" and go away from them encrazed. And the Turks will defile you and then slaughter you!

Admonishing my son, I kissed him and sent him back home, reminding him to be sure to tell Mother to come to me early the next morning. I passed the night in the field with my exiled and unhappy friends. Oh, under what mental and spiritual oppression!

* * *

It was Thursday morning, June 22. I was watching my dear wife as she hurried toward me. Suddenly two lashes of the whip fell on her tired and sweated back and stopped her, stunned. My poor wife! This was only a gently falling drop of terrible cloudbursts to come!

I approached the gendarme and in a pathetic voice said, "She is my wife. Please allow her to speak with me." This favor was granted.

We took each other's hands. Bravely she tried to control herself. I was sobbing like a child and she did not wish to increase my suffering. She had determined to mitigate my pain and console me. She had already mourned my death. But now she, though very weak in body, gathered all her moral and spiritual strength and became a brave champion. With a smile she looked at me, and steadily, with firm accents, she said, "Badveli, did you forget those sermons you used to preach? Do you not remember those divine promises which you so fervently spoke to your people for their consolation? Keep your courage. Trust in the God of those promises. Trust always. The time will come when you will again ascend the altar and testify to God's magnificence. It is necessary that you have this experience too. These are the abundant sources for your future message and ministry. Be brave!"

In truth it was a prophetess standing before me. I was inspired. My tears had dried. Now we began to speak of everything plainly—of those dangers which were threatening me after this day, of what would happen to her and the children if they were put on the road. I advised her to beg the German and American missionaries to keep her and the children. "But if this much is not possible, at least let them take the four children into the orphanage, and you set out with the baby. God knows, you and I may perish in torture, far apart. But the children will live."

After we had discussed the necessary things, she gave me a little money and victuals which she had brought with her and we said farewell—she to return to the city and I, with my friends, to sit in the field beneath the blazing sun.

A short while later some officials came from Marash and wrote down the names of all the Marash deportees who were in this convoy. Their purpose was clear. If the families of these deportees were still in the city, they too would be deported. One of the officials, who was my bitter enemy, eyed me, registered my name, and placed a special mark in front of it, that I should not be forgotten and that the deportation of my family should be certain. What unhealing wounds these circumstances were opening in my heart!

Still later Miss Schaffer, one of the German missionaries of Marash and a dear friend of mine, came to see me. She tried to comfort and encourage me. Secretly she gave me fifty Turkish banknotes, to be used for my needs and for the needs of the Armenians with me.

The gendarmes who had brought us from Baghtche were now sent back. The good Ismayale Kemal Pasha had appointed new ones and had told them that I was in this group. They had strict orders to take our convoy to Aintab safely. But beyond that, toward Biredjik, toward Der-el-Zor, the slaughterhouse, he had no jurisdiction.

How did the pasha know I was in this group? That deadly enemy of mine who had registered our names and placed a special mark before mine, in order to make double-sure of my destruction, had presented the list to the pasha. The attention of the pasha was attracted especially by the marked name. What my enemy had designed for my undoing was thus used for my advantage.

Three hours before sunset the convoy was put on its way, slowly, calmly. The gendarmes, in accordance with their instructions, were outwardly civil. All of them knew me and treated me well. Leaving behind the city of Marash, my church, the American and German buildings where my loved ones were living, my flock, the remnant Armenians, I was going forward toward an unfamiliar and uncertain future.

We moved on. A Turk driving two donkeys before him was looking for me, a letter in his hand. The missionaries had sent

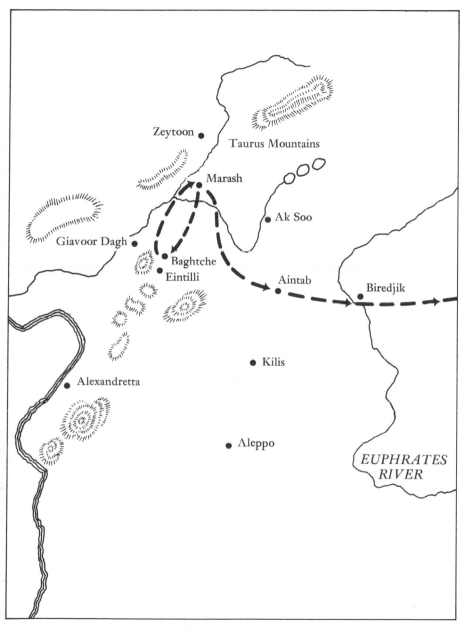

ABRAHAM HARTUNIAN'S DEPORTATION
(THE EINTILLI)

him to take me comfortably as far as Aintab. My wife too had sent me some food, a quilt, and a comforting letter. I rode on one of the donkeys and gave the other one to my friends to be used by them in turn. In this way we reached a place called *Kapï çam* (Pine Door), about three hours' distance from Marash. Here we stopped for the night.

I hired a number of other animals with the money I had so that the women and children could ride them in turn and rest on the way now and then. I also bought sufficient bread to give to the hungry.

On Friday, June 23, we traveled on. The scenes around us were horrifying. Here, there, spread out on the road, were the Armenian corpses—rotted, stinking, ugly, filling the air with horrid poison. At night we reached the place called *Kara bïyïk* (Black Mustache). Here I found a lame girl who had been left from the groups driven through previously. Who knows what she had suffered from the gendarmes! I also found an abandoned nursling, almost dead. I hired another donkey for these two, and the girl took the baby to care for it.

Next day we reached a place called *Başi punar* (Head Fountain). The baby was crying. There was nothing for it to eat. But one of our donkeys was a female and had milk in her teats. I had her milked and brought the milk in a cup to the baby's mouth. Oh! It opened its eyes wide as it swallowed the milk!

Again we saw corpses all around. This scene had become a natural part of our days. What betrayed us all again to bitter horror was the sight of an Armenian young man, lying on the ground. He had been shot but had not died. How many days had he been in this agony—hungry, thirsty, roasting under the sun by day, shivering at night with the cold? His wound tortured him constantly. No one could help him. Some of the women went near him but he was out of his mind. He twisted and turned, rolling continuously. The whole night long he rolled back and forth without ceasing, filling us all with nauseating horror. Oh that another bullet had put an end to his suffering!

Who are you, O young man? Where are your parents?
Where is your beloved? Why did you depart from your

roof? Why did you leave riches and a happy life? What was
your crime that you suffer so? I know your crime. . . .

How many thousands of Armenians were thus left in unknown places and similarly suffered and died!

The muleteer the missionaries had sent to take me to Aintab
had disappeared during the night with the donkeys. He of course
returned to Marash and told the missionaries that he had fulfilled
his mission. This was always the practice. If a deportee succeeded in hiring a horse or a donkey or a wagon, he kept it for
only a few hours. Then, together with his own goods, it was
taken away and he was left helpless in the open.

It was June 25, Sunday morning. We were near Aintab but
not permitted to enter it. We were being led to a quarry about
two hours' distance from the city on its northeastern side. It had
become the temporary dumping ground of all the deportees. The
convoys moving in this direction were always put here for one or
two days before being driven to Biredjik and then to the Der-el-
Zor slaughterhouses.

As we passed through the outskirts of the city, Turkish men
and women with glowing countenances came out to see us.
Turkish children surrounded us. They were all glorifying their
Prophet for this blessed day. But thanks to the strict guard of
the gendarmes, they did us no harm; neither were they allowed
to mock and spit at us.

I promised some money to a gendarme and, giving him a note,
sent him to the president of the college at Aintab, Dr. Merrill.

Presently we entered the quarry, called *Taş ocak* (Stone
Oven)—a large open cave, with high stone walls rising on all
sides and many caverns of different sizes dug all around. Already
there were many Armenians here, the remnants of the previous
convoys, the old, the sick, women, children. Like sheep and oxen
they had been herded into this dirty, stinking fold.

Our convoy was added to their number, and we were now a
multitude of more than two thousand. But there were many others with us, the corpses of those who had fallen from exhaustion,
hunger, thirst, or from the wounds they had received. There was
also a large horse. Unable to bear the horrors, it seems, he had

fallen in the cave, out in the open, under the sun, his carcass with the corpses of our people. His belly split open, his vitals bulging out, a nest for wasps and flies, creeping with maggots, he was infecting the whole cave with poisonous stench.

Only one way led out of this ditchlike cave of ours, a narrow cut in the rock always guarded by gendarmes. We had no bread, no water, not even a soft spot to sit on unless we chose to sit on a corpse.

Soon the gendarme I had sent came in and gave me Dr. Merrill's card, on which was written, "We will do our best for you." He received his money and went away.

Where was the lame girl now? Where was that small child? I do not know. No doubt they had withdrawn into a dark corner of the cave and, hungry and thirsty, were awaiting their death.

Where was that chaste girl from Adapazar? She had finally reached here with a thousand and one sufferings and now sat in a corner, trying to cover herself from the lustful eyes of the Turks. Armenian girls were being sought. The Turkish aghas and young beys of Aintab had to have servants. But their purpose was clear. Every time new convoys entered this cave, they immediately sent a number of their women to separate out the beautiful girls and take them to their houses. This time too these women had come and were looking around. Among others they found this girl and were taking her away. Poor girl! She had refused to be the wife of one Turk. Now she was about to be the victim of many Turks. Later I learned that the Turkish aghas and beys forced our girls into their houses, and, after having used them, they exchanged them with each other. And so many of our Christian girls became merely the lust-tool of many Turks.

A little later Turkish women came into the cave and began to shout, "*Gâvurlar, satlïk çoçuklarïnïz var mï?* Infidels, have you any children to sell? We want to buy them."

Oh, the mothers! With great difficulty they had been able to bring at least one or two of their children here, leaving how many behind on the roads! They knew that there was still a long, long road before them, and it would not be possible to bear any other burden but themselves! And they were certain that after this day their children would die of hunger, thirst, exhaustion, yea, even of heavier sufferings! Therefore the words "Have you children to sell?" sounded something like good news to them. About ten mothers stood up and, holding their children's hands, began to walk toward the Turkish women. When the children understood, they clung to their mothers and began to cry, to scream, to plead: "Mother, don't sell me! Mother, I will not leave you! Mother, I don't want to go!"

The children were screaming. The mothers were sobbing. All the Armenians watching this scene were sobbing too. I was on the verge of losing my mind. My heart was broken. Tears flowed down my cheeks.

No, the children were not sold. Mothers and children withdrew together and hid themselves, awaiting a death under heavier suffering. For during this deportation, called the Eintilli deportation, of the twelve thousand Armenians hardly one thousand escaped. More than eleven thousand died a terrible death, beginning at Baghtche and even unto Der-el-Zor.

Many of our teachers, professors, and doctors—those of the educated class—were captured and with the words "So you are the intellect of this people!" had their heads placed in vises and squeezed till they burst.

Many children were herded out to the deserts, thrown alive into ditches, and covered over with dirt and sand, to smother beneath the earth. Many were thrown into rivers or dashed to the ground. Many were killed by ripping their jaws and tearing their faces in half.

Many women were stripped naked and lined up, and, their abdomens slashed one by one, were thrown into ditches and wells to die in infinite agony. The *kaymakam* of Der-el-Zor, holding a fifteen-year-old girl before him, directed his words to a murderous band and then, throwing her to the ground, clubbed her to death with the order, "So you must kill all Armenians, without remorse."

To save bullets, many Armenians were stoned and hacked with axes.

Convoy after convoy was driven night and day unceasingly,

robbed, raped, then brought to the edge of streams and forbidden to drink at the point of the gun. Under the burning sun, thousands perished from hunger and thirst.

Many were gathered in one place and burned alive. One of these, left half dead and later rescued, told me that for days she had remained with the corpses and had lived by eating their flesh.

Verily, I cannot understand how God looked down on these scenes and kept silent.

Why the Armenian debasement? Why such heavy slavery? What nation has suffered so? Unable to endure Christ's crucifixion, the sun veiled its face. Was the crucifixion of Armenia less full of anguish or more deserving, that that same sun looked down unabashed upon the scene? My faith has not wavered. I trust and worship God. But those who, under the burden of this and similar circumstances, were broken in faith, these I do not despise. May the God of faith have mercy on them.

This day too was darkening. But even in the darkness we could not sleep and forget our suffering for a few short hours. Another herd of deportees, more than a thousand, was added to our numbers. Now everyone in the cave began to look for a husband, a child, a father. Many found each other. They kissed. They wept and made others weep. But those who did not find their loved ones here were more fortunate! I began to praise God.

And *my* family?

One of the American missionaries, Mr. Woodley, went to see the Turkish commissar, who recommended their deportation. Mr. Woodley, who I am sure did not know what this really meant, accepted the recommendation and kindly sent that same muleteer and those two donkeys which he had previously assigned to my use to the building where my family was staying. He himself came to see my wife and children off with glory and honor.

But just at the moment they were leaving the building, Dr. Vartan Poladian, one of the members of my Official Board, and at this time in military service, appeared on the scene and wanted to know where my family was going. When he learned the situation, he was furious with Mr. Woodley and insisted, *"Pampish* (the pastor's wife) and her children must not go!" He alone prevented their going.

The muleteer, taking the two donkeys and Mr. Woodley with him, departed, and my loved ones returned to their nest. Shortly my wife, my son Albert, and the baby were taken into the German hospital; the other three children were placed in the German orphanages. They were thus forgotten by the government, their deportation being taken for granted.

Dr. Merrill did his best to save me. Near nightfall he sent the *belediye reisi*, the commissioner of the city, and an Armenian military doctor, Dr. Hovsep Bezjian, to the cave, to see whether they could at least assure my safety according to law! They of course found no way to do so and soon departed.

Dr. Merrill's servant brought me a package (which he lowered from the top of the cave by a rope) with some food and a little money in it. Until now all I had eaten was bread, onions, and garlic, a small supply of which I had in my bag and used very sparingly. Now I had some cheese and a few cucumbers. I passed the night in the cave, without the slightest hope of freedom.

On Monday morning, June 26, contrary to our expectation we were put on the road again. Like a gust of wind, dozens of gendarmes entered the cave and began to lash away. The people streamed out, and the gendarmes outside began to line them up. I too went out, with my bag, my quilt, and my coat. The cave was now empty except for corpses and near corpses.

The convoy, nearly three thousand souls, started off. Where? To Biredjik, from there to Ras-ul-Ain, from there to Der-el-Zor the slaughterhouse. Every hope of escape was now lost.

Suddenly I heard a voice near me. "Badveli, Badveli, come out of the line to the edge of the road. Stretch out on the ground and lie low."

Turning toward the voice, I saw a young man in military garb. I did not recognize him. "Friend, how can I stretch out here?" I said. "In a little while the gendarmes will see me and kill me."

"I tell you to lie down here!" he insisted.

"Who are you?" I asked.

"It is not the time to question. Don't let this chance escape. Stretch out here and lie low, I tell you!" His tone was now commanding.

I found myself in a dilemma, but thinking that perhaps this was the hand of Providence, and that there was something other than death purposed for me, I obeyed. I gave all the money I had, about forty banknotes, to a friend from Marash walking next to me, requesting that he use it for the needs of the deportees since it had been given for that purpose. I gave him also my provisions and water bottle and coat and quilt. Somehow I thought I would be rescued. "Let my wretched countrymen use all I have," I thought.

As I lay down on the ground at the edge of the road, I saw two other Marashtsis lying a little distance away. And near by was a young mother with her two small ones. I knew her. I had performed her wedding, and in what splendor! She was the wife of Mesrob Bey, one of the Cholakian brothers. I watched everything secretly. There were others lying down here and there. I could hear the clamor and shouting of the gendarmes, the lash of the cutting whips, the groans and cries and screams of my people. I remained face down for three hours, beneath the scorching sun, until my compatriots were driven on and had disappeared, hurrying toward their slaughter.

Silence finally prevailed. A gendarme came and ordered us to get up and enter the cave. This time we were pushed into a dark side cavern full of corpses. More of the dead were being dragged in by ropes tied to their feet. This was the grotto of the dead, and obviously considering us in the same class, they had placed us here.

But in spite of these horrid sights I was comforted by the thought that the one who had caused me to stay here would take me out and lead me to a safe place. I waited. Who was that man? I did not know. How he had found me and why he had dared leave me here I did not know. What was to happen to me I did not know. Hours passed; my hope and comfort were being consumed, my fear and doubt were growing. I felt a kind of regret that I had heeded the voice of the stranger. Perhaps I should have gone on with the convoy. I had no food, nor money, nor anything. At length I said to the two men from Marash, "Come, let us pray that God may find a way to help and free us." Thus we

Courtesy of Stanley E. Kerr

The City of Marash

"Coming home, coming home, never more to roam"

Courtesy of Armenian Democratic Liberal Organization

Jemal Pasha

*Courtesy of American Committee for the
Independence of Armenia*

Some Were Hanged; Some Were Shot

"Corpses! Corpses! Murdered! Mutilated!"

Courtesy of Armenian Democratic Liberal Organization

Soup Kitchen in Aintab

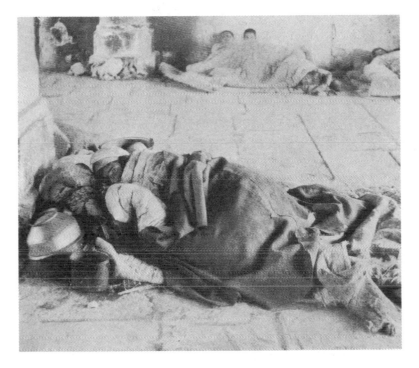

Courtesy of Armenian Democratic Liberal Organization

The Streets Were Their Homes

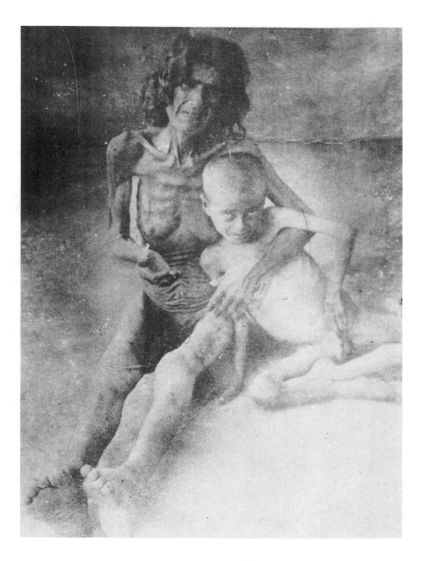

*Courtesy of Harry S. Nakashian
and John K. Garabedian*

Mother and Child

bowed our heads in the grotto of the dead and spoke to the God of the living.

A little later an Armenian young man came into the cave. He was Dr. Hovsep Bezjian's servant, Alexander by name. Thinking that the convoy had not yet gone on, Dr. Merrill had sent him to tell me there was no hope for my safety and to give me some medicines and twenty liras, with his remembrances.

I accepted the medicines but not the money, knowing that the gendarmes would soon take it away from me. I told Alexander to return the money to Dr. Merrill, to inform him of my present condition, and to ask him, if possible, to try again for my freedom. One of my friends asked Alexander to inform his mother-in-law living in Aintab that he was here, that she should bring us something to eat. This much, and Alexander departed.

Now my darkness had thickened and hopelessness was enthroned. A few more hours went by and my friend's mother-in-law came and brought us something to eat. We ate and were refreshed. Of course all who came into the cave did so only after heavy payments. Receiving permission, we came out of the grotto of the dead and sat down in a slightly more airy place. As night pressed on, I stretched out on the rocky ground and slept. At least during the hours of sleep we were unconscious of our sad existence.

In the morning we somewhat satisfied the demand of hunger with the crumbs left over from the previous day. The hours passed, and we fell deeper and deeper into dejection.

At noon another stranger came to us. He asked for me. We withdrew into a corner and he handed me a letter. It said: "Badveli, with sincere love and moved by the desire for service, I caused you to stay here, hoping in some way to save you from this den. But, after using every possible means, I find I am unsuccessful. The only thing that can be done is this: flee with the bearer of this message and enter the city and hide."

But, fearful and troubled, I said to this second stranger-friend, "Go and salute my friend. I am grateful because of his sincere love. He has done his very best for me. But I cannot escape. Therefore I must again walk the road."

He bade me farewell with deep compassion and went away. This was the hour to cry, "My God, my God, why hast thou forsaken me?"

I was alone. Closing my eyes I called on God from the depths. But this was no common prayer. God himself had come down into the cave and was numbering those sweat drops which like blood flowed from my body and flooded the very rock on which I was sitting. "Father, let thy will be done. If thou wilt, thou art able. Let me not drink this bitter cup. But if it is thy will that I drink it, help me that willingly and trustingly I may drink it."

My prayer over, the light of the Mount of Transfiguration shone on me, and I was happy. I returned to my friends and began to speak with them. The sun fell at last. Again darkness came. We were lying on the ground.

The stranger who had caused me to stay here, I found out later, was a young man of Aintab, Harootune Darakjian by name. Born in Biredjik, he now was serving in the Turkish Army as a craftsman-soldier. His brother, Bedros, had been a teacher at one of my schools in Marash in 1914 and in these last weeks had been with me in Baghtche as a supervisor over a number of laborers. At the time Bedros was teaching in Marash, Harootune had passed through the city as a soldier and, attending a service on Sunday, listened to my sermon and learned who I was. Now, during the deportations, he was keeping an eye open for his brother, and this day he had come to the cave for that purpose. His brother was not there, but he had seen me marching away and desiring to save me in some way, had persuaded me to lie at the roadside and wait. Unable to bring about my freedom, he had sent his friend, Mugurditch, to help me escape, but this too had been futile. Nevertheless, by causing me to remain, he had given another person an opportunity to save me: Alexander.

When Alexander left the cave the day before, he did not return the twenty liras to Dr. Merrill. He reasoned, "These twenty liras belong to Badveli. I will use them therefore for his freedom, because now there is no hope either from the Americans or from any other source."

First he returned to the cave and bribed the guards with the twenty liras. Then he informed the relatives of my two friends about his plan, and with them he made all the preparations for our escape. On the night of June 27, as we slept, ignorant of the escape plan, suddenly we heard footsteps. Alexander stood before us.

"What's the matter?" we asked.

"All of you get ready," he said. "We are going to sneak you into the city." He disappeared, and returned in a few minutes with a gendarme. They led us out of the cave; we were in the open air. Alexander led, we three followed, and the gendarme came after. We walked with the greatest caution through secret places. In a little while the gendarme went back to the cave. Thus by roundabout paths we reached the American hospital without meeting anyone. Alexander rapped on the gate, which opened, and pushing us inside, he vanished.

The hospital had been taken over by the government and was now full of wounded Turkish soldiers, officials, servants, and guards. Only a small building in one corner of the compound had been left to the American missionaries. It was a miracle that one of the Turks did not see us. The man who had opened the gate was an Armenian, informed ahead of time of our escape by Alexander.

I knew the campus and so we quickly passed over to the American side, where I found a native of Severek, my beloved sexton, Sister Mary's son, Hovhannes Sarkissian. He received us gladly and led us to a place of safety. He gave us food to eat, and that night he made me sleep in his own bed. My two friends were spirited away from this building by their relatives and hidden in another safe place in the city.

I had thought that my escape had certainly been planned with the knowledge and approval of the Americans. But they knew nothing about it. Indeed, rather than according me a cordial welcome and protection, when they learned that I was on their campus, they sent me a note (not coming to me themselves) saying, "You must leave our building at once. Your presence here is dangerous to us and to all the orphans in our charge."

This statement had some truth in it. They were caring for hundreds of Armenian orphans, and it would not have been right for them to protect me at the risk of these children, since strict orders had been given: "Whoever hides an Armenian fugitive-deportee incurs the immediate deportation of his family and the confiscation of his house. Foreigners too will be sentenced to punishment if they are thus unfaithful to the government." But since I had no place to go, I became obstinate. Although my escape had come about without the knowledge and approval of the Americans, nevertheless, I was now in their circle. I could either remain or go and surrender to the government and face immediate death.

For three days I simply hid. On Sunday, July 2, the same dirge was repeated: "You must leave the building!" And I answered with the refrain: "I have no place to go."

On Monday I received an ultimatum: "This very day you must leave the building!"

I did not know what to do. I was praying. I was thinking. Finally I decided to write a letter to President Merrill's wife, to try to awaken her pity and to use her kindness to good advantage. Women are more sympathetic than men and have great influence over their husbands. The result was as I expected. The next day was the 4th of July, the day of the declaration of American independence, and all the Americans were celebrating around a sumptuous table. Mrs. Merrill read my letter to them and spoke in my behalf. And finally it was decided to keep me at the college and to protect me. That night I shaved my beard and cut my hair. Wearing an ordinary workingman's *zïbïn*, I joined Dr. and Mrs. Merrill as their servant, and we three left the hospital and proceeded to the college building about a quarter-hour's distance from the city.

I entered this building on July 4, 1916, and it was on September 4, 1918, that I returned to Marash and was again with my loved ones. Thus I remained hidden here in Aintab for twenty-six long months.

8

I SHALL SET FORTH briefly the important events during these months of my college imprisonment. I spent fourteen months in the college building (after which time it was occupied by the government), and the rest of the time in the girls' school on the outskirts of the city. First I served as a proctor to about forty young men who, like me, were being hidden in the college. Then I became *Hyrig* (Father) to more than one hundred orphans.

Having much time at my disposal, I read about a hundred books from the college library. On Sundays it was my custom to lead the services which were held for the students and orphans; and every day we used to gather for prayer.

Under an assumed name I was able to correspond with my wife now and then.

Because of the famine and extremely high prices, our food was mainly bread. Only at noon we had something warm, a kind of thin soup, to go with our bread. The missionaries used to give me five banknotes (about $2.50) each month so that I could buy some other things to eat, but I sent almost all this money to my family in Marash.

All this time, the deportations went on, and every time a group from Marash passed by, my heart was full of fear lest I see my loved ones.

In Marash my church remained open. Under the leadership of the old pastor, Rev. Kevork Kasarjian, the services continued. The broken and unhappy remnant of my flock, in love and faithfulness to their deported pastor, continued each month to give a small sum to my family in order to help them live. At such a time of high costs and famine, it was very difficult for my wife to take care of a family of six. She rented a spinning wheel and began to spin cotton, to earn a little money. My son Albert learned the trade of weaving in one month and began to work day and night in the weaver's ditch to help his mother. My daughters Helena and Rosalind learned how to knit stockings and helped in that way. Despite all these hardships, my loved ones did not complain, knowing how fortunate they were.

There were always terrifying rumors that the American buildings would be occupied, that the orphans would be taken away, that the students would be forced into "military service." Many times officials came and investigated the buildings and filled us all with fear and trembling. Twice the mutessarif suddenly entered the building and began to search the rooms. At such times the students hid in corners and holes here and there. Neither time did I have a chance to withdraw from my room, and I marveled that the governor did not enter it. He passed it twice and continued on his way. I was not discovered.

In April of 1917, when the United States declared war on Germany, the Turks became hostile and insulting toward the Americans. They began to deal sternly with the missionaries. One day soldiers surrounded the whole building. We learned that they were going to take all the Armenians and either place us in "military service" or deport us—both of which signified the same thing. We were all prepared and ready. Our necessities for the journey were in our bags. One morning an official entered and asked for all those liable for military service. He took about forty students with him. I was waiting in a corner and was certainly seen. But without mentioning anything about me, he took the rest and went away. All were driven out to the desert, among them college graduates and students of theology. A few months later some of them escaped from their place of exile, but they were attacked on the way. Only two returned to the college and gave us the ill news of the fate of their friends.

A short time after this incident we were ordered to empty the college building and turn it over to the soldiers. Thus we, with the orphans, were forced to the building of the girls' school.

At this time a terrible pain began in my head, eyes, and ears, and finally I became completely deaf. For months I suffered in this way, living in a world of silent pain, but with time I regained my hearing and the pain subsided.

The deportation, famine, high prices, and various epidemics of these years were working great havoc in Aintab. The stories from other places were heartrending, but the story of the Armenians of Aintab and its surroundings was no less terrible. The remnants of the deportees, driven from distant regions and scattered throughout Aintab and its environs were subjected to unendurable hardships. Already they had walked long, long roads, had lost their loved ones, had been beaten, had been ravaged by hunger and thirst. Now they were clothed in filthy rags, blackened, smelling, rotting. They slept on the streets. But what was worse, Turkish hoodlums would not leave the unprotected women and girls alone. In the darkness of night especially there was every form of rape. Hundreds of women like these, with their children, used to come to the American building every day to receive some food and relate the daily dishonor and disgrace to which they were subjected. The harems of Aintab were full of Armenian women and girls snatched from the convoys. One had succeeded in placing her son in our orphanage, and now and then she used to come to see her child. She told me her story. Once married to a refined and wealthy young Armenian, she had lost her family, her mother-in-law, father-in-law, and husband. All that she possessed had been taken away from her, and she had been forced into the slavery and shame of the harem.

One day a young Armenian mother entered the gate of our building. She had four children with her—one of them a suckling pressed to her breast, the other three perhaps four, six, and eight years old. She sat near the gate, her back against the wall. It was winter, snowing heavily and bitterly cold. She and the children were shivering and their teeth were chattering. They had come to beg a piece of bread. How had they lived until now? With what indescribable sacrifice and suffering had this mother kept her children! The orphanage could not help them. I took my dry bread for that day and gave it to them. The children snatched it from my hand and began to eat it voraciously. The mother did not partake of it. She went hungry.

True, I was in the American circle and comparatively safe. But my anxiety about my loved ones, the endless and hellish work of deportation, the daily sufferings to which the remnants of my nation were subjected, the fear of new evils to come—these were heavy burdens and already I was bending beneath the load. I was worn out and diseased in body and spirit.

I wish to relate the stories of two Armenian children.

One day a boy of ten came to the orphanage carrying a box of vases, saltshakers, waterpots, birds, banks—made of the white soft stone of Aintab and exceedingly beautiful. Here indeed was an exposition of fine art, and all of us were attracted by it. The orphans gathered around the lad, who wanted to sell these articles for a few piasters each.

"Who made these, my son?" I asked.

"I did," he answered proudly.

"But you do not have any tools. How did you make them?"

"I have one tool, a small penknife, and I use that."

"And why do you make them?"

"To earn my living. I do not like to beg. My parents taught me that begging is an evil thing, and that even in the most hard times, I should try to earn my bread with the labor of my own hands. I have lost my parents. I have lost everything. But I keep my parents' words. During these days of deportation, wherever I went I determined not to beg, and in every place I found a means to live by; here I have found this. It is not fitting for an Armenian to beg."

I praised and encouraged this lad and bought a number of articles from him. Here again was an explanation of why the Armenian burns but is not consumed, why he falls but does not die.

A small Armenian girl was taken into the house of a Turkish

bey as his adopted child. Every means was used to make her forget her parentage and Christianity. Her name was changed to a Turkish one, and she was instructed to offer the *namaz*, the Moslem prayer. But this little girl continued to speak Armenian. She knelt and she prayed, daily making the sign of the cross. When she was threatened, she answered, "I love Christ. My mother told me that Christ is our loving savior."

They tried to persuade her with gifts and promises, but it was impossible. Then they flogged her and imprisoned her in dark places—to no avail. Finally they told her, "Do you see that large, savage dog? If you do not do as we say, we will put you in his den at night and shut the door and he will tear you to pieces." But the little girl was willing to be shut up in the den with the dog.

At night they put the child and the dog together and closed the door. In the morning, to their amazement, the dog was lying quietly on the ground, watching with open eyes, and the girl, her head on the dog's belly, was sleeping. When they saw this, they said to one another, "We must not trouble this child any more for she is a little prophetess."

A great calamity during this time was the curse of denial in Syria, issuing from the command of Jemal Pasha. Jemal Pasha had ordered all the remaining Armenians under his jurisdiction to desert their faith and embrace Islam. This pasha, who, in comparison with Talaat and Enver, seemed rather kind and conscientious, perhaps had thought thus to save the remaining Armenians from annihilation. But despite the fact that his motive was good, the deed itself was evil. Many Armenians in Hama, Homs, Damascus, Beirut, and Aleppo, and the districts surrounding these cities, accepted his offer and survived.

The *hocalar* propagating this movement—the emissaries of the order—came to Aintab too. Another terrible hour of trial was before us. We gathered secretly and prayed. We encouraged each other. And we pledged to remain faithful to Christ even till death. But fortunately the order was not carried out in Aintab, and we remained unmolested.

One day someone brought me a letter. When I opened it and saw the signature, I began to shake all over, and with trembling lips to pray to God. The signature was that of Aram Bey, one of the Cholakian brothers. Mentioning me by name, he had written, "One of our friends is sick. We are sending him to you. Place him in the American hospital and have him attended to."

How had they sent this letter to me? How had this messenger, traveling from such a distant place as Giavoor Dagh, come here safely? If this letter had been discovered by the government, not only would I have been raised on the gallows, but all the orphans would have been driven away and the Americans would have been expelled from the country. Fortunately for us all, the man never appeared. Perhaps he died on the way.

Beginning July 18, 1918, the American Army took the offensive, and the Central Powers, including Turkey, were defeated. The deportations ceased, and the pressure placed on the still living remnants was lightened. There were even rumors that the deportees would be allowed to return to their homes.

My wife, weighed down by loneliness and by her heavy toils, and encouraged by the hopeful situation, wrote asking me to find some way to return to Marash. She herself appealed to the German missionaries and besought their help to bring me home. German officers and soldiers, together with the Turks, were continuing their military operations in Marash. The Turkish soldiers, under the supervision of German officers, were transporting timber from Marash to Biredjik, to build boats on the Euphrates River. On Sunday, September 1, a Turkish soldier and a German officer came to me with a letter from Miss Schaffer, my faithful friend and benefactor. I was to trust these men, she said, and go with them to Marash. Following her advice, I set out next day and on Wednesday, September 4, walking through secret paths, entered Marash as a fugitive. After an absence of twenty-six months, I joined my family.

But the danger was not yet over. The war was still going on. The deportees were not yet permitted to return. Miss Schaffer advised me to remain hidden in my house and not to resume my church activities. I was unable to wait, however, and the very first Sunday after my return I entered my church and with enthusiasm delivered God's message to the remnants of my flock.

About a week after my return to Marash another American

attack took place and the enemy lines were shattered. And two months later the armistice was signed—on November 4, 1918, with Austria, and on November 11 with Germany.

Now we felt free and safe. The Turkish Army was in retreat. All the civil officials were fleeing. Especially those Turks who had done much evil against the Armenians were fast taking to their horses and disappearing from the city. The Armenian houses that had been occupied by the Turks were being emptied and given back to their owners. The Turks who remained in the city suddenly began to act with humility and sweetness toward us. A little before the armistice Beirut, Damascus, and Aleppo had been occupied by the victorious English Army, and in consequence the Turks already appeared half dead.

The liberator of Turkey, Mustafa Kemal Pasha, narrowly escaping from Aleppo, came to Marash and prepared to flee to the Turkish provinces. The Armenians had begun to smile, the Turks to droop. I had rented an Armenian's house before the war. It was still being used by a Turkish military officer, but when I appealed to the government, asking for its evacuation, my house was quickly given back to me.

Thus the war came to an end, and 1919 began.

PART THREE

1919—1922

9

IT WAS THE FIRST MORNING of the year 1919. The New Year service was being held in my church, before a great audience. Praise, tears, smiles, joy, and sadness were intermingled. Whatever else it was, this was the morning of Armenia's resurrection. A new era was about to begin.

The deportees who had survived were gradually returning to Marash, and with the passing days and weeks our hopes were growing that the British troops in Aleppo would soon come and occupy Marash too.

Yet on February 28 another massacre was planned by the Turks. In Aleppo, almost under the eyes of the British Army, many Armenians were slaughtered. The British came to the rescue, but it was too late. Although the massacre was curtailed, the terrible fact remains that Armenians had been murdered in the presence of the British Army. We in Marash were once more thrown into fear and confusion. To laugh, to boast, to be joyous was not, it seemed, our inheritance and right. We were terrified that the same massacre would break out here, and in truth the Turks had changed their attitude and assumed their former bloodthirsty, threatening ways. Fortunately this uncertainty and fear did not last long. In the early days of March the British forces occupied Aintab and then Marash. We poor

Armenians, credulous as always, and inclined to flow like water in every direction, revived, our hope and enthusiasm rising again. The troops entered Marash on Saturday, March 8, with no opposition whatever, in glory and splendor, even bringing with them, in their military wagons, hundreds of Armenian deportees. What great happiness to us! What pain and grief to the Turks!

Sunday, March 9, was a day of celebration. My church was crowded to the doors. During the service a wealthy and well-known Turk, Ibrahim Hoja, came in. He approached me with a smiling countenance and firm steps and asked to have an opportunity to speak a few words to the congregation. Invited to the pulpit, he said, "Islam is a corrupt religion; Christianity is true. I knew this difference long ago and was a Christian in secret. I am redeemed by the blood of Christ. But I never dared reveal myself. I was afraid of the savagery of my own people. Now I am happy. I glorify God for this day of freedom. I congratulate you and I pledge to remain with you always. May the Lord bless you."

When we heard these words, our joy and hopes were heaven-high. It seemed as if all the wounds, open in our hearts for years, had suddenly healed, that the gloom of former days was now no more! I held out the hand of brotherhood to Ibrahim Hoja in welcome, and I was sincerely happy that the door was finally open for the Christianization of Islam!

After the service my campus was filled with the Armenians of the city, with groups of orphans, with songs and the earsplitting din of a band! Even the British officers mingled with the multitude. The children were singing! The young people were dancing!

This day had been set aside for the hanging of the bell. During the war all the church bells had been melted down and used for military purposes. For a long time the bells had been silent. My church had had a large new bell brought from Germany and kept the old one hidden. The new one had of course been seized. Now we were about to bring the old one from its place of hiding and raise it on the bell tower. The bell was drawn up amidst thunderous applause, and for the first time since the war it began to ring with a sweet-sounding voice, and to fill the whole city with hope. Our convert, Ibrahim Hoja, whom we called Brother Abraham, was the happiest and most zealous member of this celebration. Like David, he was dancing before the Ark of the Covenant!

The British national anthem was sung. There were speeches. The British troops were praised. And the celebration ended at a late hour.

In a short time the National Armenian Union was organized, and I had the honor of being one of its first members. Zealously we worked at the task of taking care of the returning deportees. Those who had no homes, or no place to go, were settled wherever possible. Those from the villages around Marash and from Zeytoon, little by little, were sent back to their homes in small groups. Schools were reopened. Once more the people busied themselves with their trades. In all, the returned deportees numbered twenty-five thousand, and the churches, streets, and houses of Marash were filled with them. Someone looking at this multitude and this activity would have thought that Marash had suffered no harm from the war. Everything was as before, going on regularly and happily. My church alone had more than two thousand people; during services the building was always filled to overflowing, many standing outside at the windows to hear the Living Word. Besides Ibrahim Hoja eleven other Turks, among them a *yüzbaşi*, accepted Christianity, and the Turkish Christian Church opened in Marash with twelve members. The able Rev. Abraham Berberian was appointed pastor of this new church, which became recognized officially as the Fourth Evangelical Church of Marash.

For years no weddings had taken place, but now day after day was occupied in the performance of this holy sacrament. The priests of the city and I, now the only ordained pastor of the Evangelical community, were in a sense making up for the empty years.

The British troops had begun to put up buildings in the city and to repair the road from Marash to Aintab to Aleppo, thus making traveling easier. This was the year of freedom, happiness, enlightenment, and reward for the Armenians. The past had already been forgotten. There was nothing to worry about for the future. The present was very bright and we were deluded into thinking it would go on always.

Beginning in September, 1918, immediately after my return to Marash, my left arm had been paining me. Nevertheless, I continued with my daily work until the pain grew so severe that I could no longer move my arm easily. In the early part of 1919 my arm became entirely useless; during the pronouncement of the apostolic benediction I was forced to raise only my right arm. I feared that my left arm was paralyzed permanently.

On May 3, 1919, I was weak, but I performed two more weddings and then went to the Conference of the National Union. There my beloved friend and a member of my official board, Dr. Vartan Poladian, saw me and was troubled. He felt my pulse, took my temperature. I had a fever. "You must go home and get to bed," he said.

I obeyed and with heavy steps, my head throbbing, I reached home and got in bed. During the night my fever rose. On Sunday someone else preached in my stead. The doctor kept coming to examine me. On the fourth day he said, "You have typhus fever and must be moved to the hospital."

On Thursday, May 8, I was taken into the German hospital, which now was occupied by the American Red Cross. Head physician and supervisor there was that well-known and good-hearted lady, the American Dr. Elliott. I remained in the hospital until Thursday, August 14—more than three months. For a time all hope for my life was abandoned. All the hardships I had suffered during the previous years had combined and brought my body to this terrible pass. But Dr. Elliott spared neither time nor effort nor expense to save me. With her fine care, and the prayers of my friends, loved ones, and church I passed through this illness too and once again began to live. And the marvelous thing was that all my ailments, including the pain in my arm, which had lasted a whole year and caused my paralysis, disappeared, and I became healthier and stronger than before!

In the early part of September the president of the Near East Relief, Dr. Barton, and one of the missionaries of Constantinople, Dr. Gates, had visited Marash with a number of friends. I had several interviews with them, and at one of our official meetings the general of the British forces was present. There was an exchange of opinion about the present situation, about the possibilities for the future, and about the cause and freedom of the Armenian nation. But the attitude and words of these friends were depressing rather than encouraging. We Armenians returned to our houses with a sense of foreboding. Our laughter and joy were but for a moment. Dark and terrible days still awaited us.

We were now living in a few rooms in one of the buildings on my church campus. The German missionaries and their families had been expelled from Marash and all the German buildings were under the administration of the Near East Relief.

From September on, the political atmosphere of Marash showed radical changes. The British officials and officers became very friendly with the Turkish officials and aghas of the city. The Turks became immediately hostile toward the Armenians. In the city and the nearby villages, on the roads here and there, Armenians were again being robbed and killed; and the British, except for official formalities, took not one concrete step against these crimes. Whenever we appealed to them, asking them to protect us, they would confiscate some guns from the Turks in order to appear officially concerned, but in a few days these were secretly returned.

Soon the Turkish government openly began to distribute firearms and ammunition and other military equipment to the Turks of the city and the surrounding villages. Every Turkish house became a military center. Every Turk was armed. Still the British kept silent, assuming the role of spectators. The pasha at this time, Atah Bey, an able, clever, cunning man, exploited his friendship with the British officials and made all these preparations, not only with their consent, but with their secret encouragement.

One day a number of Zeytoontsis, traveling from Zeytoon to Marash, were attacked on the road by a Turkish band, and seven of them were killed. On another day, in the village of Jamooslu, six Armenians were slaughtered. On yet another day three Armenians going out from Marash to their vineyards were shot by the son of a well-known agha of the city. Another traveling Armenian was tied to a tree and shot.

When we called these crimes to the attention of the British

officials, they invariably replied as the Turkish officials were accustomed to do: "Yes! We will look into it! We will investigate! We will punish! Such things do happen! Don't be afraid! Everything will be well!" But nothing was done.

Autumn came and our national schools were opened. The poor common people, ignorant of the calamitous situation near at hand, tried zealously to make up for lost time. Meanwhile Mustafa Kemal Pasha was organizing his rebellion in the districts of Sivas and Angora, and everywhere, even in Marash, his spies were busy. The Turkish aghas and common people, informed of this movement, were happy and prepared accordingly. The pasha of the city was fanatically at work to organize the revolution well. The British, well aware of the machinations, were not only careless but actually encouraged them, showing Mustafa Kemal and the Turks ways and means and supplying them with armaments. Britain and France had begun to quarrel over the occupation of Cilicia—under whose mandate should this territory be?—and the British, knowing that they were about to withdraw from these parts, were encouraging the Turks to strengthen themselves so as to make things difficult for the French!

Oh that we had realized from the start that all the European powers were thinking only of their own gain and were ready to sacrifice the Armenians!

Oh that we had known they were not our saviors, but murderers more cruel than the Turks! They had not declared war to save enslaved and powerless nations but to buy oil, mines, and land by giving these same nations in exchange!

Oh that we had understood they were deceivers! They had not prepared to preserve the peace of the world but to preserve their own imperialism at the price of the peace of the world!

Oh that instead of relying on them and respecting them we had relied on and respected the Turk! The Turk openly declared himself our enemy and destroyed us. The European, Judas-like, kissing us, betrayed us. The Britisher, the Frenchman, the German, the Italian, the Russian—all the Christian powers of the world are our murderers. The Armenian nation must not forget this fact. Always, from century to century, from generation to generation, from mountain to mountain, from east to west, she must cry out, "The Christian powers of the world are the murderers of the Christian Armenian nation!"

The blood of the Armenian will protest to the God of justice! And either the result will be our murderers' repentance, and perfect, just compensation for the Armenian fragment, or else the thunderbolt of righteousness of the just God will strike Europe and destroy her! I believe in God. I believe in justice. And I know that of these two, one will come to pass!

* * *

My son Albert, desiring to receive a college education, set out from Marash on Friday, September 26, for Tarsus. After many difficulties he was accepted by the American college of Tarsus, whose president then was Dr. Christie.

* * *

Thinking that the opportune time had come, the missionaries and churches of Aintab invited the pastors and delegates of the surrounding districts to Aintab in order to reorganize the annual conference of the Union of the Armenian Evangelical Churches. From Wednesday, October 1, until Tuesday, October 7, we pastors, ministers, and delegates were occupied with the sessions of the conference. When the delegate from the Turkish church, Patlak Zadeh Mohammed Effendi, presented his report, all of us arose and sang the Doxology, sincerely happy that the hour for the Christianization of the Turks had arrived. And in truth this would have been the fact if the Christian nations of the world had not turned Mohammedan.

On October 8, returning from Aintab to Marash, we passed the night with a group of British soldiers who had encamped near the city. There was a hushed rumor among the soldiers: "The British troops will withdraw from these parts." We had expected as much, and now our hearts were troubled.

After a meeting with all the Armenian leaders, we appealed to the British general, desiring to learn of the situation from him. He answered with typical British stoneheartedness: "Yes, we are going to leave."

"But what will happen to us?" we asked.

"I don't know," he replied, adding that if the people wished, they could leave the city by joining the withdrawing troops. What an offer! Just returned from deportation, having recently rebuilt his nest, hardly having breathed a satisfying breath with his children, the Armenian was again to leave everything and follow the British troops on foot! And where was he to go? Where was he to stay? No assurance was given about that. "Let the people follow the withdrawing troops!"

This news spread throughout the city and the villages with the swiftness of lightning. The Turks were in glee; the Armenians went into mourning. Now the Turks openly declared that if the British withdrew they would massacre all of us! Already a long list of Armenian names had been prepared. As soon as the British were gone, these people would be hanged on the gallows.

How could we protect ourselves? The French troops were in Adana. Quickly we sent a report to the French, revealing the situation to their general and beseeching him to send troops to Marash before the British withdrew, to protect us who had been betrayed to die. Wretched Armenian! As one murderer leaves he invites another, so that the massacre left incomplete by the first should be completed by the second!

Our request was granted. The French troops, among them many Armenian volunteers, would soon arrive in Marash. The Turkish aghas and a number of officials, terrified by the supposed vengefulness of the Armenian volunteers, fled to Albustan. Once again the Turks began to tremble and the Armenians were joyful.

On Wednesday, October 29, the French troops, with the brave Armenian volunteers as a vanguard, victoriously entered Marash. On Saturday, November 1, the British withdrew. The French occupied the important centers of the city and placed their cannons here and there. Different sentry groups, composed of Algerian, Tunisian, and Armenian soldiers, were organized and, under the leadership of French officers, undertook to protect the peace of the city. New troops kept arriving and the French Army was strengthened.

One week! Only one week! Again the Turks were humbled,

the Armenians proud. The Armenian changes his color very quickly. He forgets his yesterday. He is easily deceived by the sheen of the present. Yet once again we were to be deceived.

On Saturday morning, November 8, as the Armenian volunteers, under orders, were patrolling the city, suddenly a gun was fired from a Turkish mosque and one of the volunteers fell dead. This was an experiment on the part of the Turks, to learn what the attitude of the French would be. It was expected that the French would immediately rise up in protest, arrest the criminals, and raise them on the gallows. Nothing of the sort. The corpse was removed. The next day it was the stupid, short-sighted Armenians who staged a pompous funeral procession, to the anger of the savage Turks! It seems that we excel in lowering our dead into the grave with magnificent pomp! Oh, we were symbolizing what the Christian powers were about to do to us: they would give us too a magnificent funeral service!

The Turks were not questioned about this incident. It was hushed up and forgotten. But they had found out what they wanted to know, and now the martial gusts began to blow.

But what did the French general do? He called the Armenian leaders to him. He encouraged us. He advised us to keep silent and to act with prudence. "Don't be afraid!" he said. "I am here in the name of the Alliance to protect you with all my power! France will protect her honor. She will not allow her face to be spit at! Be confident and instill confidence into your people."

Again we were deceived. These lying words filled us with hope, and we inspired our people too with hope.

A few weeks later we heard that a governor was coming from Adana to take over the government of the city from the pasha— an official by the name of Monsieur André. How happy we were! What the general had said was true! The French were occupying both the military and the civil centers!

On his arrival, surrounded by hundreds of Turkish and Cherkess gendarmes, Monsieur André was received ceremoniously in the governor's room, then with great pomp came out of the *konak* and was led to a building especially prepared for him. With him always was the Armenian representative, Monsieur Vahan.

After resting a few days, Monsieur André and Monsieur Vahan undertook their duties. They placed French officials in the government offices. When they saw that on Friday, according to religious demand, the Turkish flag was unfurled over the fortress in the center of the city, considering this an insult to the French victory they ordered it taken down and the French flag hoisted in its place. Everything was going from glory to glory!

The following Friday the French flag instead of the Turkish flag was waving over the fortress. How proud we Armenians felt! But our pride and the French honor had but a few hours to endure. At noon the Turks were gathered in the mosques to offer *Cuma'a namaz*. But the prayer was not offered. The *hocalar* had received a revelation from Allah: "As long as the flag of Islam does not wave over the fortress, so long will it be impossible to offer *namaz*."

Now, divinely stirred, the crowds rushed out of the mosques and daringly ran toward the fortress, in the view of the whole city, of the Armenians and the victorious French forces, under the very eyes of the French general who had said so haughtily, "France will not allow her face to be spit at!"

The French flag was torn down and the Turkish flag raised. Then the Moslems returned to their mosques and, with the deep calm of assuaged conscience, offered *namaz*.

The French general; the French troops; Monsieur André, the governor; and our Armenian, Monsieur Vahan—all kept silent. The Turk had spit into the face of the French, had defeated the French troops. His fear dispelled, he was now growling victoriously!

A few days later, as Monsieur André and Monsieur Vahan were entering the government building, the Turks attacked them. Monsieur Vahan was thoroughly beaten; Monsieur André expressed his respectful thanks to the Turks that they had not been so impolite as to beat him too. On the second day after this incident, these champions, André and Vahan, whipped their horses and disappeared from the city.

All this time the Turkish aghas of Marash were not merely sitting and waiting in Albustan. They had broken away from the sultan and were in conference with the *çete-a-bed*, Mustafa

Kemal, to whom they had sworn allegiance. Already one of Mustafa Kemal's men, Kuluj Ali Pasha, had been sent as a *çete-a-bed* to Bazarjuk, a village about six hours' distance from Marash, where he was organizing the revolutionary movement against the French, together with Arslan Bey, a Circassian who had joined him. All the surrounding villagers, be they Turks, Kurds, or Circassians, were armed and ready to fight. In the same way the Turkish people in the city were armed and were waiting to battle with the French forces when the opportune time should come. Military centers were being established and filled with supplies. Trenches and ramparts were being constructed. These things were being done openly, in the very presence of the French officials, officers, and troops.

The French, finally sensing danger after it was too late, began to prepare and organize themselves. Ammunition and artillery were brought, and new troops entered the city. It was evident that in a short time Marash would become a battlefield.

We Armenians rejoiced secretly, certain that a clash of this type would end favorably, with the crushing of the Turks. Our great worry was that our countrymen settled in Zeytoon, Fundejak, Geben, Derekeoy, and their environs were in danger of being massacred. Whenever we appealed to the military officers, they, gulping down bottles of wine, and with dizzy heads, would say, "Fear not! Only two hours are enough and we will crush the Turks and assure eternal freedom for the Armenians."

Again and again we were deceived, and again and again we believed the things that were promised us and felt encouraged. Thus we had begun the year 1919 with doubts and confusions, and we continued it with uncertainty, living a life half free, half enslaved; sometimes hopeful, sometimes hopeless; now happy, now sad. The only difference with previous years was that we called this the year of Armenia's freedom—a freedom that was a mixture of slavery, terrors, and sinister future expectations. The year 1919 ended as it had begun.

10

THE YEAR 1920 was a most terrible and blood-stained year—the year of the last massacre of Marash; the year the horrors left undone by the World War were consummated; the year when the six thousand Armenians of Hadjin were annihilated, when one hundred and sixty Armenian girls were taken from the American girls' seminary in Hadjin, brutally raped in the Turkish harems, and then massacred, when Hadjin itself was destroyed; the year when all the Armenians in the villages around Marash and fifteen thousand Armenians of Marash were slaughtered; the year when all the Armenian churches, buildings, and shops were turned to ashes; the year when nearly three thousand Armenians on the road from Marash to Adana were buried in the snow and died; the year when hundreds of Armenian volunteers, betrayed by the French to the fire of the Turks, were killed; the year of slavery and hardships for the ten thousand Armenians who barely escaped from the hell of Marash's war; the year when the decree was signed for the annihilation of nearly a thousand Armenians of Zeytoon who had remained alive; the year when the Armenians of Aintab suffered the nightmare of a long internal conflict; the year when new massacres were planned for the Armenians of Merzefoon and its surroundings; finally, the year when the Turk again spit into the face of the French.

In the first days of January the French forces were increasing day by day and occupied the various centers of the city. Three hundred French soldiers were stationed on my church campus. We found them very hungry and right away went from house to house to gather food and feed them all.

The French were preparing to quell an approaching rebellion, and the Turks were preparing to start one. What should the Armenians do? Certainly they would side with their liberators! So they in turn were preparing too, under the protection of the French, to fight against the general enemy.

On Friday, January 16, the Turkish aghas and religious leaders called a meeting and invited the Armenian aghas and religious heads, myself included, to consider the present delicate situation and if possible find a way out of the crisis. We went to this meeting, held in *Ooloo Jami*, and were treated very kindly indeed. Even tea had been prepared in our honor. But soon the mind of our hosts was revealed: "We request you Armenians to unite with us, your Turkish fellow-countrymen, and to fight with us against the French, force them out of the city, and then to live with us in eternal brotherhood."

Would that we had accepted this request! It would have been a much wiser course than the one we took. At least we would have lived! But could the Armenian have held a position contrary to that of his emancipator? And could he have united with one who had always been his murderer? Thinking that if we accepted this course of action we ourselves would wound our savior-army, we refused, and the meeting dispersed.

The governor, Atah Bey, had by now organized the Turkish populace in every way, made all his preparations, and was getting ready to withdraw from the city. With perfect cunning and artful politeness, he called on all the Armenian leaders to say farewell. On Saturday, January 17, he left the city, having appointed in his stead the *tahrirat müdür*, the secretary of the city, a notorious man from Kilis named Mohammed Bey.

On Sunday, January 18, all our churches were crowded. Although we were threatened with war, yet when we considered that there were six thousand French troops in the city, that cannons were entrenched on every side, that six hundred brave

Armenian volunteers protected us, we were encouraged and happy. Next day, the Armenian Christmas day, was celebrated as never before.

On Tuesday, January 20, the French general peremptorily ordered the Turkish government to dismiss all officials and to hand over to him all the government buildings with all their departments. The Turkish officials did not reply. On Wednesday morning the general had the representative of the governor of the city and four other Turkish officials of the first rank arrested. After questioning them, he imprisoned them. The representative, however, promising to persuade and prepare the Turks for uncompromising obedience, was soon set free. The other four remained locked up. The kindling wood had been arranged and was ready. Only a spark was necessary to start the blaze—and behold, the French general had supplied that spark!

At one o'clock in the afternoon of Wednesday, January 21, 1920, the firing began. The city of Marash was now a battlefield. The Turks had taken the offensive and unexpectedly opened fire on the French and the Armenians indiscriminately. French soldiers and Armenian men, women, and children were in the streets and, unable to reach their houses or military centers, fell where they were. In a short time the streets were littered with corpses.

There were seven safe military centers in Marash: (1) the American girls' college; (2) the German (Bethshallum) orphanage; (3) the German hospital; (4) the Armenian Catholic Church; (5) the Latin monastery; (6) the Gregorian Church of Forty Children (*Karasoon Manoog*); (7) the First Armenian Evangelical Church (my own church). Almost half of the Armenians, about ten thousand, managed to take refuge in these centers; the rest had been left in their houses or in a number of unprotected church buildings. The Armenians from the Armenian quarters, about twenty-five hundred in number, were in their church building, the Church of the Holy Virgin, without any protection whatever.

The Turks were battling madly, attacking, shooting, massacring, sparing no one. The French from the very beginning assumed the defensive. They would open fire here and there, without at all harming the Turks, only preventing their advance upon them.

This very morning a few hundred Armenian volunteers had left Marash to go to Adana. We did not then know why. But my sincere belief is that they were sent away by the French to appease the Turks. The Turks of the city especially hated these Armenian volunteers and many times had appealed to the French to get rid of them. The truth is that the French betrayed the volunteers to the savagery of the Turks. Attacked by overwhelming numbers of *çete* holding the roads, they were murdered horribly, except for a few who escaped and reached Adana.

The Armenians in the surrounding villages, all but the Zeytoontsis, were that same day annihilated by the mobs. The Turks had sworn their greatest oath not to spare a single Armenian, not even suckling babes. Children were ripped open before their parents, their hearts taken out and stuffed down their mothers' throats. Mothers were crucified naked to doors, and before their very eyes their small ones were fixed to the floor with swords and left writhing. The fight was between the French and the Turks, but it was the Armenians who were being killed.

All these horrid messages reached the French general. But he, drunk with wine, would curse vainly, would deceive us, and would use the time for his own advantage. Recalling his words that in three hours he could quell the rebellion, we waited anxiously. But the day ended without his taking one decisive step. Mustafa Kemal's men—Kuluj Ali and the Cherkess Arslan—were already in the city directing the rebellion and massacre. Their purpose was to break the French power and to annihilate the Armenians relying on that power. And the French defended only themselves, not at all concerned about defeating the Turks, unoccupied even with the thought of the safety of the Armenians.

In the buildings on my church compound were three hundred French soldiers and about two hundred fugitive neighbors. Since we were now in the very heart of the battle, the officer in our center dispersed his troops here and there for protection, not so much of the Armenians as of his own soldiers.

Night pressed on. We heard the firing of guns unceasingly,

the shouts of the attackers, screamings and wailings. Above this turmoil there came suddenly the terrible supplication of an Armenian woman who had been left in the street and in the dark had come to the door to find safety. As she entered she was shot by the French soldiers, who thought her an enemy.

During the evening the French officer began to talk secretly to his men. He was figuring out a plan in his mind. What was this plan? To take his soldiers, slip out of the place, and join the soldiers in the Armenian Catholic Church, another stronghold, because our center was dangerous and the other one was safe. Chivalrous France thus leaves the weak behind to be massacred! She flees to save herself!

We could not have prevented the French from abandoning us, but Providence took a hand. As the soldiers were leaving, the Turks, who now had manned every nook and cranny and were prepared to shoot in any direction, instantly, saw them and opened immediate fire. A few soldiers were shot, and the officer, convinced that escape was impossible, returned to the building abashed and distributed his troops to their former places. All night the shooting continued. We had no rest or sleep.

On Thursday, January 22, the officer called me to him, and we walked around the campus to ascertain the dangerous spots and to observe the surrounding houses so that the soldiers might be arranged accordingly. As we were making these investigations, it happened that in one room I was standing before a window. The officer was a little distance from me, to one side. An Armenian young man was standing behind me. The officer, with the foresight of a soldier, sensed danger, and taking my hand drew me a few steps toward him, away from the window, saying, "It is dangerous to stand there." Hardly had I changed my place when an enemy gun was fired. The bullet found its mark, and the young man behind me fell wounded to the floor.

That day, that night, and the next day passed in the same way. Neither the soldiers nor the people had anything to eat, but I brought out the great supply of provisions stored up in my house for the winter, and all were fed day by day.

On the night of January 23, to the firing, the thundering of the cannons, the din of battle, a more calamitous evil was added

—fire! The Turks had begun to set Armenian houses and buildings on fire. Even Turkish buildings were being burned if it seemed possible thus to spread the blaze to the Armenian quarters or one of the military centers. The flames rose everywhere; the city glowed beneath their light. From every side, bullets were incessantly whizzing like hail, and no one knew when he might be hit. Every moment there was danger of a fierce attack on any center where the Armenians had gathered. The fire horrified us. It was impossible to withstand it. I do not know a battle on a field or in the air, but I do know that a battle in a city is a hellish thing!

In the other centers the situation was the same or even worse. But no horrors can ever parallel the experience of the Armenians in the Armenian quarters and in their houses. These were tortured without respite and without pity and then slaughtered. A well-known and supposedly good-hearted Turk, Murad Bey, was in the Great Mosque, *Ooloo Jami*, where the murderers were at work. Some Armenian women and children, watching the slaughter and awaiting their turn, pleaded, "Please tell them to shoot us and not cut our throats with the knife!" and our kind Turk answered, "Don't be afraid. The knives have been sharpened well and you will not suffer much."

The city's greatest Hoca was there too, *Dayï Zade Hoca*, and the Turks turned to him saying, "*Hoca*, shall we slaughter the small children too? Does the Koran give us permission?" "Yes," he answered, "slaughter them too. The Koran permits. We must kill the offspring of the scorpions, too, that they may not grow and sting us."

Let me not forget to say that *Ooloo Jami* was very near the Church of Forty Children, around which four thousand French soldiers had encamped.

There was an Armenian section near our church, called *Kooyoojak*, where many families, not having an opportunity to escape to any center, had remained and during these five days defended themselves. The Turks now resorted to burning them out. But because they could not get near an Armenian house, beginning a few houses beyond they set fire to Turkish houses, and the flames spread into the Armenian section. The whole section was soon aflame. What great wealth was there, all of it turned to ashes! About a thousand Armenians, under cover of night, holding their children's hands, fled noiselessly, crawling on the ground; some reached our center and some the German orphanage.

By Sunday night, January 25, our buildings and campus were overcrowded. There was almost no place to sit down; there was no place to sleep. There was nothing with which to cover oneself. There was little left to eat. The children cried. The mothers were heartbroken. The men were pale. It was a hellish sight!

Some tried to escape to the Catholic church not far from us, but the Turkish bullets prevented them, after a few had been shot. A mother with three of her children tried to escape. One of the children was shot and fell to the ground. She returned to our building with the other two while her wounded daughter, stretched out on the road, began to cry, "Mother, I am shot and am dying. Why do you leave me here?"

Our houses and possessions were no longer ours. My family and I huddled together in one corner of a room—like all the rest. Oh, how unbearable it was to see this, my poor nation's new and heavier burden, to see my wife and children trembling, awaiting their doom.

On Monday, January 26, the officer, alarmed by the fire of the previous night, thought that a few Turkish houses near the church might soon be occupied by the *çete*. He therefore determined to burn them to prevent that danger. This was perhaps the only wise thing our French officer did. But unfortunately, as the flames from those houses rose, sparks blown by the wind reached the wooden bell tower of my church and set it on fire. With our own hands we had seriously endangered ourselves. How could we put this fire out? The Turks saw what had happened and now directed their bullets at the bell tower. Thus, unable to climb up the tower, we decided to cut it down by sawing its four pillars from the bottom and tumbling it over into the yard with ropes. Quickly the whole structure came crashing to the ground and the fire was put out.

The officer comforted me, saying, "Don't worry. We will rebuild that tower for you. And this time in stone! And more magnificent!" Alas! Not only did the French not rebuild my bell tower but they reduced my church and all the buildings on my campus to ashes!

Tuesday, January 27, was the fatal day for the Church of the Holy Virgin. As I have mentioned, twenty-five hundred Armenians had taken protection there and with a few light arms had defended themselves these few days. The Turks were working systematically and one by one removing the enemy forces from their midst. Already all the Armenians who had stayed in their houses and sections had been annihilated. The *Kooyoojak* quarter had been burned to the ground, and today this church was surrounded by thousands of savage, bloodthirsty Turks. While bullets hailed against the building incessantly to prevent the escape of anyone, they brought kerosene in large cans and sprayed it on the walls on every side with pumps. Pieces of sackcloth, soaked in kerosene and lighted, were thrown on the building. Flaming rags on the end of long poles were raised toward the roof. The Armenians inside were panic stricken. They shouted, screamed for help. They waved flags in every direction. But there was no help. The French general viewed this scene through his field glasses and kept silent. A few steps away, nearly four thousand French troops were watching. The handful of Armenian volunteers left in the city pleaded with their commander to be allowed to save their countrymen for whom they had come far distances. But they were ordered, at the gunpoint, to stay where they were and not to intervene.

The mournful supplication of the Armenians now rose to heaven, and God's angels too did not come to their aid.

The building caught fire. The flames roared upward. All the people were consumed, and in a few hours one could see there only a smoking heap of silent ashes. Twenty-five hundred persons had been destroyed—to the glory of the French, and to the heartbreak and horror of the remnant Armenians.

For the rest of the week the same monstrous deeds were repeated. The continuous sound of gunfire had terrorized us. We were not just walking toward death; we dwelt in death. Death had besieged us, and no matter where we turned, it threatened to strangle us. The fire, the sword, the bullets clawed at us.

To these terrors were added hunger, thirst, filth, sleeplessness, and disease.

The Turks had blocked the water running to the church fountain. Its flow had been like teardrops, but at length it began to bleed: the blood of slaughtered Armenians trickled from its spout.

The French soldiers were still safe in their places. The Turks had no fear of them because they knew the French would not attack them. It was the Armenians who everywhere, every time, in every way, were forfeiting their buildings, churches, schools, houses! And what use was it to keep them? Not one Armenian would be left to live in them.

Now the time had come for the Turks to attack the military centers, take the French soldiers prisoners, and kill the remaining Armenians. On Saturday night, January 31, they concentrated on the Catholic church. Under a rain of bullets the school building of the church was set on fire. It went up in a sudden blaze, the flames lighting the whole city. There were about three thousand Armenians in the church and about five hundred French soldiers. The Armenians manifested great courage. At the risk of their lives they tried to save at least the church building and the other large buildings on the campus. A number of them were shot. But they kept on bravely and succeeded in limiting the fire to the building where it had started.

What about the French forces? Did they perchance fear the Turks? Never! They had six thousand troops, guns, cannons, and ammunition. Everything had been in perfect readiness. Had they wished to take an active part, the Turks would have been quickly crushed. Why did the French do nothing? I do not know. I am not a European diplomat. But as an Armenian and a simple lover of my nation, and as a man of religion, I believe the French Army came to Turkey to camouflage the annihilation of the Armenians by the Turks. Having performed that duty faithfully, having finished its work well, it went away.

Monday, February 2, was a day of panic in our center. I was with my family in a corner of the school building adjacent to the church. There were many other families with us. Suddenly we saw smoke. The building had been set on fire with kerosene-soaked rags wrapped around long poles and set aflame. Our young men immediately set themselves to try to extinguish the blaze, but it had been set from the outside and to go outside was impossible because of the barrage of bullets. The only possibility was to dig a hole in the wall from inside and put the fire out in some way through it. But as preparations were being made for this endeavor, we were ordered to leave the building and go into the church because the fire was spreading. With many others, my wife and I, holding the children's hands, entered the church. All the people had crowded in there, while the brave young men were trying to contain the fire. The Turkish gunfire became suddenly fiercer. From every side there was a storm of bullets, hand grenades, and shells. Death's gaping mouth seemed ready to swallow us all at once. At this point the French soldiers received orders from their officer to be prepared to escape. Their bags were on their shoulders, their guns in their hands, and they were ready to flee. And we, what were we going to do? Who told you, friend, that the French soldiers came here to protect you? You are an Armenian, and your lot is to be massacred!

My children began to cry, sensing that the hour of death had come. I abandoned all hope, convinced that we would all now perish. Weeping, I gathered my wife and children close and said to them, "This is the last hour. We are all going to die. But in a little while we will be together in heaven."

Oh, now I knew the shattering of the spirit, the lacerations of the heart, the insufferable anguish of those parents who with their children had passed such hours as this, and who then perished.

When we saw that the fire had not yet been put out and that the attack was growing more intense, in desperation we ran out of the church to an empty Turkish house near by. A bullet whistled through the air just an inch from my eldest daughter Helena's head, but we reached the house and hurried to the cellar to await our dark fate. Our veins had been drained of blood! The color of our cheeks had gone! We were like those who have come out of the grave. We were living death's-heads.

And then came the good news! The fire had been put out! Stealthily we returned to our nest, this time occupying a place on the first floor of the school building in the middle of the campus. And there we rested.

During the twenty-three days that the battle lasted there were hard and heartbreaking tasks: finding food for about a thousand people, providing them with water to drink, removing the garbage and rubbish and preventing the spread of disease. The dead had to be buried, the wounded treated, and those who had lost loved ones consoled. I myself was in need of consolation and encouragement; how could I console and encourage others? But the God of comfort helped me and comforted me and used me to help and comfort others. Within the bounds of possibility I kept order among the people to assure a semblance of calm. I made a list of all the people, family by family, and once a day some kind of food—or at least something that looked like food—was prepared in large caldrons and distributed to the people, just enough to keep them alive. The grown-ups bore it patiently but the children were always crying. They wanted more food than we were able to give them. If the battle had gone on longer than twenty-three days, the people would have died of hunger, if not from other causes.

Across the street from our compound was a building in which about one hundred girls were living under the supposed protection of the Near East Relief—girls who had been recently rescued by the English from the Turkish harems. Now they were abandoned in that building with their housemother, Mrs. Gohar Shanlian. The only man there was the doorkeeper. Since the fighting had begun without warning, no arrangement had been made for these girls. How many times I had told our French officer, "Those girls are in danger. Let us bring them to our compound during the night." But the officer paid no attention to me and left the girls to their sad fate. Their building was attacked on Thursday, February 5. Their housemother and doorkeeper were shot, and all of them were taken out of the city and given as payment to the Turkish soldiers, who raped them cruelly and then massacred them.

On Friday, February 6, the seventeenth day of the battle, a French airplane flew over the city dropping notes to the military centers. New French forces were coming; the freedom of the city was assured. Freedom! But for whom? Assurance! But for whom? Who was thinking of these questions now? Was there any need for such niceties? Freedom and assurance for all! For the French and for the Armenians!

Woe, deceived Armenian! Ever deceived and ever wronged! There was freedom, but not for us. Freedom for the French! But for us new shedding of blood, new burning in the fire! We were once again to be sacrificed for someone else's freedom! Nevertheless, this day we were happy, ignorant of the fact that the command to retreat had been given and that the French were preparing to flee.

Again the Turks tried to set our building on fire. But as the long pole with its flaming rags was raised toward our roof, a French soldier took aim, and the man holding the pole rolled on the ground wounded. The rest of the Turks ran away. Bravo!

That night the French soldiers left our center and were replaced by about one hundred Armenian volunteers under the command of a few French officers. Airplanes and new forces and arms had by now reached the city. But they had not come to punish the Turk, to save the Christian; they had come to save their own soldiers besieged by the Turks, to take them away and abandon the remnant of Armenians to the massacring hordes. Long live French diplomacy!

Saturday, February 7, was reminiscent of Saturday, August 7, 1915, when hell's harbingers ran through the streets ordering all men seventeen years old and above to gather outside the city for deportation! This was the day my parsonage and magnificent church were turned to ashes, the day all my possessions were consumed by flames, the day my library, my books, my sermons, my labors of twenty years were destroyed.

The Turks were ready to challenge even the new French forces—of course to our bitter destruction! They had determined at any price to set my buildings on fire today, and because no other way was possible, they would burn a tall Turkish structure near by, so that the flames from there might reach us. I knew that this Turkish building would cause us trouble. How many times I had begged the officer to burn it on a day when there was no wind. But he never heeded me. Now, with a north wind blowing, the flames gradually advanced to the parsonage. It was impossible to stop them, though the brave Armenian young men did everything they could. I prayed continually that at least the church might be spared, but my prayer did not find acceptance in heaven.

We all withdrew to the two buildings situated in the middle of the campus and watched the burning of my parsonage and then of my church.

Night came on. The people were betrayed to more hardships. There was no room to sit down. Sleep was out of the question. There was now nothing to eat. The French had with them a number of mules which they slaughtered, and we chewed on this tough flesh, almost raw and unsalted.

Next day, physically, mentally, and spiritually almost overcome, we regarded the sad scene of the destruction of the fire. Our condition was now more perilous since the enemy could easily attack. No wall or ramparts had been left.

We had felt somewhat encouraged by the presence of the few French officers and the Armenian volunteers, but this very night there were hushed whisperings among the latter. All of them were afoot. They were making their preparations.

Utterly exhausted in every way, the people slept where they could, in cramped discomfort. I too slept. The Armenian volunteers were our protectors.

Suddenly, near midnight, someone shook me and whispered to me to follow him. I went out on the campus to see that all the Armenian quarters of the city were aflame. All about was the terrible conflagration. And more terrible than this: there were neither Armenian volunteers nor French officers! Betraying us to the sword of our murderers, they had quietly stolen away. My God! What cursed days we pass through one by one! What now? It would not do for me to merely bewail this calamity, to show despair and drive others to despair! I would do my very best even under heaven's curse itself!

I called together a number of the Armenian young people, each of whom had a gun. Stationing themselves here and there, they fired their guns intermittently, so that the Turks might think the French were still with us.

Monday, February 9, was one of those days which the imagination cannot comprehend. If the Turks had been aware that the French forces were withdrawing and our center had already been abandoned to its fate, our annihilation would have been the work of one hour. But because the French cannons, both in the city and outside, had begun to bombard the centers where the Turks were thought to have gathered, our enemies retreated to safe places. Thinking they were now really being attacked by the French, they had no time to pursue their attack on us. For the moment we were safe. Moreover, from somewhere had come encouraging words (I do not know who had falsely planted the seeds!) "All the military strength is being centralized for a united and powerful attack to crush the Turks once and for all!"

Accustomed as we were to being duped, in truth it was good that we were deceived now. At least the heaviness of our day was lightened by this deception. For once the successive thunder of the bombardment and the omnipresent whizzing-rumble of machine-gun fire sounded pleasing to our ears.

The Turks were apparently completely convinced that the French were serious and would strike, ruin, avenge. They began to tremble and grow pale. All their houses were immediately vacated, and the women and children were sent in groups to the surrounding villages. The unarmed men too departed. The fighters hurriedly withdrew to their secret centers. Ah, let the French troops play at formality and bluff! Yet this one step had daunted the vehemence of the Turk. His morale was broken by a straw. The Frenchman was victorious in retreat. The Turk was defeated in fear. This in itself is perfect evidence that even on the first day France could have crushed the Turk, if this had been her purpose. But the Frenchman was toying with the Turk while the latter mercilessly harassed the Armenian, to the great amusement of the Frenchman! If France had desired, even today she could have occupied the whole city and meted out just punishment. But the Turk was dearly loved by the Frenchman.

It was Tuesday, February 10, the day of Samaria's plenty and luxury! The Armenians from the other centers who had survived, learning that the city was now evacuated by the Turks, rushed out from their imprisonment and began to help themselves to everything they could carry out of the empty Turkish houses. They soon reached our center with the news, and our people too ran for booty. In a few hours our two buildings were filled with food, clothes, house furnishings, etc. I was displeased by all this. I did not move from my place. Although the cannons were roaring and the Turkish attacks had ceased, nevertheless, my heart was not satisfied. I had no inner assurance of safety. I did not like this conduct of my people. But I could not have prevented it.

The whole day passed in this way. At nightfall, as if to avenge the deeds of the Turks, the Armenians set mosques and Turkish houses on fire and killed a few Turks they found here and there. Again the Armenians were joyous and were congratulating each other. Even those who had lost their parents, children, husbands, were smiling, and the woe of fifteen thousand dead countrymen was quickly forgotten. Why, in the Latin monastery a band was playing, giving us the good news of Armenia's freedom! One would think these people were trying to say in their own simple way, "If the losses we have sustained have brought the defeat of the Turks and the freedom of the Armenians, it is good!" Would that at least this had been so!

At midnight it was snowing heavily and the earth was thickly covered. The air was bitter cold and windy. The cannons still roared. The machine guns rattled. Suddenly there was a towering blaze and a crepitation, and then terrific explosions. The great Turkish barracks where the French troops had encamped was aflame!

This was enough to explain everything. The French forces were withdrawing and they themselves had set the barracks with all its contents on fire. I realized the situation immediately, but what was there to do? It was impossible to go out from our center and join the soldiers. I trembled. I waited. Death and annihilation were now both imminent and immanent for us!

Those Armenians who were near the soldiers and who had learned that they were withdrawing went with them. In all nearly three thousand men, women, children attached themselves to the French and left the city, on foot, in the blizzard! All this time the cannons outside the city kept up their bombardment, to prevent any Turkish attack. But later we learned that these bombs were all shot into the hills without causing any damage to anyone or anything.

Wednesday, February 11, was the birthday of my little boy, Vartan. He was five years old. I had nothing to give him. I kissed him as he slept that morning and shed two teardrops on his head. It was very probable that this was the last day for all of us.

The richest and most influential family of the city, the Khurlakians, and some others came together to think what should be done in the present critical situation. These people had shown much respect and given great honors to the French and were especially hated by the Turks! Could not the French at least, in gratitude, have informed them of the withdrawal, instead of leaving them thus to their savage enemies?

They were now asking, baffled, "What shall we do?" Some suggested running after the troops and joining them. I myself did not consider this wise, saying, "The troops have been gone for some time. It will be impossible to catch up with them. By now the Turks are aware of the situation and will massacre all of us on the way."

Already we knew the fugitive Turks were returning, group after group. I suggested our staying here. But was it safe? No! Just as dangerous. However, here at least we would be protected from the snow and the wind, and from the exhaustion of the journey. The others did not agree with me, and so they set out immediately. Alas! What I had feared came to pass. These fleeing hundreds of Armenians were attacked and murdered. Only a few, wounded, half-dead, horrified, found their way back to us.

Since our center was in great danger, I thought it best to go to the other center near by, the Catholic church, and join whoever was there. Although this was a perilous undertaking, we had to attempt it. Leaving all the booty behind and holding the children's hands, we slipped along secret trenches, in and out of dark corners, through holes, and reached our destination.

Now we were about five thousand, from moment to moment awaiting attack. That night we took down the French flag which was still waving over the building and hoisted a Turkish flag.

There was a French flag over the building of our center also. In the darkness I went back there with a few friends, and we took down the French flag and returned safely.

It was Thursday, February 12, the twenty-third day of the battle. Today the verdict would be pronounced for our destruction or our rebirth. We were all hungry. My children were crying for food. There was nothing to eat here but an abundance in the center we had left. I was foolishly daring enough to take my niece Yester, a girl of twenty-five, back with me to our former center. There we cooked some pilaf and, putting it in a pan, started back. Hardly had we taken three steps out when this former center was occupied by the Turks. If we had remained there a few more minutes, both of us would have been killed. When we reached the Catholic church, we saw that already it was being surrounded by the *çete* and *başibozuk*. We were the last ones to enter, and the door was locked. I placed the food before my children without telling them anything about the urgency of the situation. They began to eat happily.

Now the remaining two buildings of our former center were set on fire, and the flames rose toward heaven. Preparations were being made to burn all of us too. Guns were trained on the building from every side to prevent any escape. Kerosene was being sprinkled on the walls. The poles were ready with soaked rags aflame on their tips. Loved ones embraced and kissed each other in tears. One more minute and the flames would devour us! All hope was gone. Some were praying to God with uplifted arms, either for freedom or for faith to die in the faith!

At this ghastly moment salvation came to us. A voice outside shouted, "Open the door!"

I ran to the door. "Who is it?"

"We!" answered someone.

It was the voice of saving angels—the American missionary, Mr. Lyman, and one of the Near East Relief officials, Dr. Wilson. I flung open the door. White flags in their hands! Gendarmes with them! We gathered them in. When the mob outside saw these people, it abandoned its murderous plan. The Armenians, condemned to death, began to smile.

These brave souls, seeing that the French had treacherously

withdrawn and that the remainder of the Armenians were betrayed, had had daring enough to go out into the streets and to appeal to the *çete-a-bed*, Kuluj Ali, to Arslan Bey, and to the Turkish aghas. Their intercession was fruitful, and the Turks agreed to spare us on condition that we hand over our guns and promise obedience. Five persons were chosen, among them myself, and under the protection of gendarmes, we went to present ourselves to the *çete-a-bed*. After twenty-three days of war and imprisonment, this was my first walk in the streets. But oh! What a horrible scene! Corpses, large and small, corpses of men, women, children, soldiers, littered the snow-covered ground. Even carcasses of animals were scattered all over. The snow was red. Another Armenian section was in flames. Armed Turks prowled everywhere like bloodthirsty wolves.

Finally we reached the building where the *çete-a-bed*, Arslan Bey, and the Turkish aghas had gathered. We humbled ourselves before them. We expressed our respect. They dealt with us arrogantly and rudely, while we, like guilty slaves, answered their questions slowly, fearfully, and with bowed heads. Our unforgivable crime was forgiven. Protection was promised. We were asked to surrender our guns and to obey all orders. We of course gladly promised to comply with their wishes and departed. Under the same protection, we then visited the other centers to pass on the good news of salvation and peace.

As long as chivalrous France with her great power was protecting us, we were murdered. When she departed, the Turk had pity and spared the remnant.

What happened to the Armenians who fled with the French? For four or five days about three thousand men, women, and children walked and walked, hungry and thirsty, through deep snows, in the cold and wind. The old, the children, the weak, the exhausted dropped and were left buried in the snow. They froze and slept the sleep of death. The rest, after a thousand and one sufferings, reached Adana. On the way, more than half of the three thousand were lost. Of those who got to Adana, many were taken into the hospitals to have their frozen hands and feet amputated.

On Friday, February 13, the Americans, the gendarmes, and

I visited all the centers, collected the guns, and delivered them to the Turks. On the same day, by permission of Kuluj Ali, my wife, my children, and I were received into the American circle. We washed, changed our clothes, ate a hot meal. The president of the college, Miss Blakeley, gave us her personal room to rest in.

Now the important task was the care of the ten thousand remaining Armenians—to give them shelter, clothing, food, and work. The American missionaries and the Near East Relief officials—Miss Blakeley, Miss Ainsly, Miss Hardy, Mr. Lyman, Dr. Wilson, Mr. Kerr, Miss Trousell, Miss Buckley—like angels sent from heaven dedicated themselves to their work with perfect self-sacrifice, sympathy, and unceasing efforts, struggling night and day to keep this remnant alive by any means and at any price. They recognized me as one of them and we worked together. For two weeks the people remained hidden in their centers and the necessary help was given through these centers. After that we settled them in the American buildings and the Armenian houses near by—those that had not yet been burned. Thus every building and house were crowded with Armenians.

For two years the Near East Relief continued its help. It provided money and work for men and women so that soon many were able to earn their own living. It opened schools so that the children could resume their education. It took all the new orphans into its orphanages and cared for them. Ten thousand Armenians were thus able to live, only because of the aid of the Near East Relief.

Later other workers were sent by the Near East Relief—Miss Matter, Miss MacIntyre, Miss Reid, Dr. Genaway, Mrs. Genaway, Mr. Genaway, and Mr. Stanley; and more missionaries arrived—Mr. Woolworth, Miss Rackman, and Miss Reider. These good-hearted people united their efforts and kept the remnant alive.

*　　*　　*

A short time after the terrible days of the war a military man, a *binbaşï*, Eurphan Bey of Aintab, came to Marash to substitute for the mutessarif. He was kind and conscientious and showed much regard for the Armenians. But a number of malevolent Turkish aghas, eternal haters of Armenians, began to despise this man and to work against him. Although the war had ended, these vengeful Turks continued their secret crimes; during the first few weeks after the Armistice, about fifty Armenian young men were murdered and many Armenians were arrested and imprisoned because of this or that trumped-up accusation.

About this time I and the other religious heads and Armenian aghas were ordered to appear at the criminal court for trial. We were all members of the National Armenian Union. The statement of our accusation was thus: "*Maraş harbïna sebebiyet maddesinden dolayï mütehhim.* Accused because of responsibility for the civil war of Marash." We ourselves, it seems, had hatched the Marash war! Of course it was clear what the punishment for such a crime would be! Death! Anyhow, for the Armenian there was no lighter punishment than this!

Some of my friends were immediately arrested and imprisoned. Although I was not imprisoned at this time, nevertheless I passed each day in fear.

For a long time we had not heard from Zeytoon. It was now the end of March. The governor, Eurphan Bey, and one of the representatives of Mustafa Kemal Pasha, Jemal Bey, summoned me and some of my friends and ordered us to go to Zeytoon to persuade its people to hand over their guns to the government and promise obedience.

At this time there were in Zeytoon about one thousand Armenians in all. Our well-known, brave Cholakian Aram Bey was their head and general. All through the terrible Marash war, Zeytoon had suffered no assault. Aram Bey's name was sufficient to keep Turkish forces and Cherkess enemies away. Even the Turks in Marash were afraid to attack and so the government was trying to lead the lion into the snare by using us as a means. Zeytoon had through time immemorial been a thorn bush for the Turk. During the Great War he had uprooted it and thrown it aside and breathed freely. But now again, in the same place, this cursed bush had taken root and was coming to life. Although its thorns were not as sharp as before, still it was a thorn bush! The peace of the Turk was disturbed, and unless he again uprooted it and this time burned it, never to spring up again, he could not rest! What made him especially uneasy, what wounded his pride, was the fact that when all the other Armenian villages had been burned down, Zeytoon was still standing with its brave men.

Of course I could not have refused to carry out this order, so, taking with me two laymen and an illustrious Turk, Kadu Zadeh Haji Effendi by name, I directed my way to Zeytoon. We arrived on Sunday, March 28. From a Turkish village near by I had previously sent a letter to Aram Bey informing him of our mission and requesting him to receive us courteously and to deal with us prudently. Aram Bey acted accordingly. Mounted on his spirited white horse, he met us with his followers and with the utmost politeness directed us to that beautiful parsonage which had been built especially for me, and in which I had lived for two years. Food, rest, service—everything was perfect. We ourselves opened the conversation. He and his men listened willingly and answered civilly. They set free several Turks whom they had imprisoned. They returned to their owners a number of animals which they had taken from them. Then they brought a few guns and handed them over (of course keeping a great many good ones). They promised obedience and won the heart of the agha. And we, successful in our mission, returned to Marash. Kadu Zadeh expressed himself most favorably about the situation of Zeytoon, and the matter passed over quietly without resulting in any calamity.

In 1915 Zeytoon had been set on fire and reduced to ashes. Only about fifty houses had been left on one side of the city, along with the Turkish barracks. The Zeytoontsis were now living in the barracks and in these houses.

Just at this time the Armenians of Sis, having left everything behind, were fleeing to Adana, and the Armenians of Hadjin, left helpless, betrayed to the merciless paws of the Turks, were being torn to pieces. Therefore it was not the moment to be concerned about Zeytoon. For the present at least, until the other Armenian strongholds were annihilated, the freedom of Zeytoon was granted. The Zeytoontsis were permitted to go to the outlying villages to buy and sell, and to travel as far as Albustan and Marash. Would that we Armenians had but a small part of such Turkish policy and cunning!

The French had been routed from Marash. Now the Turks, especially Mustafa Kemal and his *çete*, encouraged by this easy victory, determined to drive them out of Aintab. Kuluj Ali and his *çete* had gone to Aintab to start their work. Meanwhile the Armenians of Aintab, having learned their lesson from Marash, had moved to the Armenian sections of the city. Not one Armenian remained in the Turkish quarters. The Armenians were also well armed and had by now a good supply of ammunition and provisions. Communication between them and the French was uninterrupted, since there were no Turks between the two encampments. They had decided to remain on the side of the French and to fight against the Turks.

On April 1, 1920, peace in Aintab came to an end. The civil war of Marash had been transplanted there. But the Turks were very unhappy because they were unable to find the Armenians unarmed and to slaughter them unsparingly. Why was there not an immediate attack on Zeytoon? Partly because the obstacle of Aintab had to be removed first.

Hardly a week after the start of the fighting in Aintab I was again summoned by the government. This time I was to go to Aintab and persuade the Armenians to unite with their Turkish countrymen to drive from their common paternal soil the treacherous French. Henceforth Turks and Armenians would live together in brotherhood and perfect freedom, since the battle of Marash had proved that siding with the French was dangerous for the Armenians.

I had to obey. Accompanied by the Gregorian priest, Der Sahag, and the Catholic priest, Der Khoren, we started for Aintab on Thursday, April 8, with twenty infantrymen and ten cavalrymen and a *yüzbaşï* as guards. At the same time the governor telegraphed to Aintab, "The *Sulh Komisyon*, the Peace Commission, is on its way."

After camping the first two nights in villages, on the third day we reached Aintab. About ten cavalrymen from the city met us, and we entered the city with great pomp. The roofs and streets were crowded with people, giving each other the good news, saying, "The Peace Commission is here to pacify the city!"

The chief of gendarmes and his cohorts surrounded us respectfully and led us to the *konak*, where we partook of a sumptuous feast prepared especially for us. The mutessarif and all the civil and military officials and Kuluj Ali Bey himself came to greet us. Then, guarded on every side by gendarmes, we went to return the greetings. The Turks lined up in the streets and even stood at salute as we passed by. When I entered the room of the *çete-a-bed*, Kuluj Ali Bey, he hugged me and kissed me on my cheeks. The savage *çete* standing around were amazed at this sight.

In the evening, after a magnificent dinner, we were taken to a hotel suite. When we were alone, I turned to my priest friends and said, "Lloyd George! Clemenceau! Wilson!" What great men we were! How cunning the Turk! How politically astute! How ingenious! The Armenian, how naïve! How foolish! How presumptuous! The Armenian talks, proclaims, is puffed up, does nothing! The Turk works secretly, without words, is discreet, serpentine, but wise!

The situation of Aintab was in every way like that of Marash. Guns! Attacks! Firing! Upheaval! Noise! Death! The only difference was that the Armenians were not being massacred. The French and the Armenians were firing on the Turks, and the Turks on these two factions. Aintab was a true battlefield. We were on the Turkish side. Among thousands and tens of thousands of Turks, three Armenian religious heads! Three young men in the furnace of Nebuchadnezzar!

April 11 was Easter Sunday. After an interview with the officials, Ali Bey and the Turkish aghas, it was decided that we three intermediaries should pass over to the Armenian side and carry on our mission. I wrote a letter to Dr. Merrill and sent it across by an aged Armenian who was being used as a go-between by the Turks and the Armenians. The letter informed Dr. Merrill of our coming to their side in a short time. The answer assured us they were ready to receive us, so the firing ceased and we were soon on the Armenian side.

The Armenians had thought it proper that we carry on all our negotiations in the presence of the two American missionaries, Dr. Merrill and Dr. Lorrin Shepard (Dr. Shepard's son). They knew very well the deception of the Turks, and as representatives of the Armenians they said to us, "It is impossible to come to an agreement with the Turks. We cannot trust them. They want the Armenians to join them so that they can murder them."

Our own honest conviction had been the same. However, we requested that the missionaries at least come with us once to the Turkish side so that we might have an interview all together. Dr. Shepard did not choose to go across, but Dr. Merrill agreed to do so.

We three Armenians returned to the Turkish side, met with the Turkish officials, and set the time and place for the meeting with Dr. Merrill. Then on Tuesday, April 13, again passing over to the Armenian side, we brought Dr. Merrill back with us. At the place appointed, a session was held with the Turkish officials and the leading men of the city. There were long-drawn-out deliberations and exchanges of opinion. We spoke on ways and means of solving the difficulties. It was very clear that the Turks of Aintab did not desire to see their own city in ruins like Marash and hoped to bring the war to an end. But the *çete-a-bed*, Ali Bey, drunk with his victory in Marash, wanted to win a victory here too and establish even greater fame for himself. Thus he was opposed to anything that smacked of an agreement between the two sides and was holding fast to the conviction that the Armenians should join the Turks and drive the French out. However, Ali Bey was not present at our session, so a kind of inner agreement was arrived at without him.

It was decided: (1) The Turks, the French, and the Armenians would remain in their quarters. (2) Attacks and firing would cease promptly at 9:00 P.M. this day. (3) Sentry groups composed of Turks, Armenians, and Frenchmen were to keep guard in the three centers for the general peace, thus establishing confidence and trust among the common people. (4) The final decision by the higher authorities of Mustafa Kemal and the French General Gurro, in Beirut, would be awaited, so that matters could be settled peacefully by arbitration.

Dr. Merrill assured the Turks that he would be able to convince the Armenians and the French to act according to these conditions. The Turks personally accepted the conditions, and thus things seemed to be solved in an unexpectedly smooth manner.

Three documents containing the conditions were prepared, to be signed by the three sides, and it was agreed that this very night, at nine o'clock sharp, armistice would begin.

The meeting ended. Dr. Merrill, taking two of the documents with him, returned to the Armenian side, and we, as bearers of a great triumph, went to our places with pride and satisfaction.

After supper we were led to the magnificent parlor of the *Tekke Şeyh,* the religious head of the Turks of the city, Mustafa Effendi. Eagerly we waited for the hour of nine, when all the firing would cease and peace would be restored. As nine o'clock struck, there was a sudden terrifying upheaval! Attack, firing, the roaring of cannons—an unparalleled pandemonium which seemed to seal the doom of Aintab.

"What has happened?" we asked each other.

The mutessarif came to me and said, "You see, your men did not accept the agreement and opened fire on our men!"

I answered, "Mutessarif Bey, you know and I know who the offender is. But what's done is done. There is now no way out. Only be good enough to return us quickly to our city!"

The matter was clear. Ali Bey, dissatisfied with our decision, had led a new attack on the Armenians and thus had ruined our agreement. Peace was again destroyed. With bowed heads we went to our rooms, where we passed the night with many a perplexed thought.

On Wednesday morning, April 14, in accordance with the wishes of the mutessarif, we again passed over to the side of the Armenians. This time the Armenian soldiers opened fire on us. The Catholic priest, Der Khoren, was almost shot. The Armenians were saying in effect, "Don't come again to deceive us!"

Nevertheless, we reached the Armenian side safely, again to interview the two missionaries. They told us that at nine o'clock the previous night Ali Bey's *çete* had attacked them and been driven back. And they added, "Whatever the Turk does is deception! Agreement is impossible!"

In utter dejection, and this time full of fear, we returned to the Turkish side, informed the mutessarif of the final answer we had received, and besought him to set us on our way at once. Followed by the thunder of the continuing battle, we set out, and on Friday, April 16, reached Marash. We presented the report of our failure in bringing peace—to the great displeasure of our Turkish friends.

The civil war of Aintab lasted eleven months. From the point of view of length of time, the condition of the Armenians of Aintab was hard indeed. The difficulty of sustenance, the terrors of every succeeding day, the unceasing firing both night and day! But in comparison with the Armenians of Marash, they were fortunate because they were not left helpless in the hands of the Turks.

At the beginning of March, 1921, the Turks, defeated, fled from Aintab. Many of them came to Marash, including the general of the Turkish troops of Aintab, Miralay Salahaddin Pasha, with his soldiers. And now we were clearly told that if the French came back to Marash we would all be killed or deported!

Salahaddin Pasha had under him ten thousand regular troops. By this time the *çete* movement had ceased and it was the regular army that was fighting. Mustafa Kemal was the absolute ruler over Marash, as over many other cities.

* * *

During the last eight months of 1920 we ten thousand Armenians left in Marash lived without any definite and actual persecution. But we knew we were slaves and we remained in this condition. We were forbidden to go out of the city. Places in the suburbs—vineyards, gardens—were no longer ours. We dared not enter the Turkish quarters; whoever entered there never returned. Even in the market-place Armenians hesitated to appear for fear of being beaten. Several Armenian houses which had not been burned during the war were, during these days of "peace," set on fire. Even one of the Gregorian churches still standing and the only Armenian Evangelical church left were set on fire. Unprotected women and girls were abducted and raped. At night every Armenian was a prisoner in his house, and visits had ceased. Sometimes there was terrible gunfire in the city, the purpose of which was to terrify the Armenians. Those men who were able to work did so in their homes. Few carried on their business in their shops.

The kindly Eurphan Bey, suffering the punishment for his love of the Armenians, was removed from office and sent to Angora. He was succeeded by the inebriate and licentious Mustafa Remzi Pasha.

During this time the Turks cultivated the friendship of the American missionaries. Mr. Lyman, always taking me with him as interpreter, used to call on the officials and the Turkish aghas, and they in turn called on him. Putting in a good word here and there for the Armenians, Mr. Lyman helped us a great deal.

In the latter part of this year the Turks began to enlist the Armenian young men and to use them as craftsmen for military purposes.

Besides my many other activities I preached twice each Sunday in two different centers of the city, giving my people spiritual consolation. The Armenian Catholics and the Armenian Gregorians also carried on their religious services.

And so this bitter and calamitous year of 1920 also came to an end.

11

THE FIRST THREE MONTHS of 1921 carried on the fearful conditions of the previous year. The war of Aintab was still going on. To the evil Turkish officials of Marash another one was added, Tartar Commissar Shevket Bey, a man who seemed the very devil incarnate!

In the spring the war of Aintab came to an end, with victory for the Armenians and the French. In Aintab, at least for the present, the Armenians were breathing freely. In Adana too the Armenians were living a relatively free and peaceful life.

Shevket Bey, the diabolic Tartar commissar, became a veritable Pharaoh in Marash. He turned into lead the yoke of the enslaved Armenians and began to use them mercilessly to build his Raamses and his Pithom. This man planned to erect new buildings for the government on the wide grounds of the *konak*. But he would do it without increasing the government budget, by having the Armenians do the work and pay the expenses! To this ingenious plan the civil and military officials gave their consent. So, during the last nine months of 1921, every day hundreds of my wretched people were driven to the working quarters under the lashes of gendarmes' whips and were used cruelly without receiving any pay or food. Each man had to take his own food with him and had to labor from morning till night. The Armenian houses which were still intact were torn down and their timber was used in the new buildings. But this was not all. There was need of more timber and other building materials. These were bought from Turkish merchants and the bills were sent to us, the Armenian leaders.

We were sorely troubled. We had neither the means nor the liberty to work and so to earn money. The people were already living on relief, and with what deprivations! And now to work for the Turkish government without wages! Where were we to find the money to pay these bills sent us day after day?

During this time the Turks were not on very friendly terms with the Americans. They despised them and openly scorned them because they had not used their influence against the French, as the Turks had hoped. Therefore any intervention which the Americans might make for us was entirely fruitless. Both the government and the Turkish people were using every means to drive all foreigners from the city, and especially the Americans. The hospital that was in the hands of the Near East Relief was occupied. The largest of the orphanage buildings, where five hundred Armenian orphans were being taken care of, was also occupied, the children turned out into the streets; we were therefore obliged to crowd them into our other orphanages. All the valuables of the occupied buildings were sent to the houses of the Turkish officials.

Until now some of our grammar schools were open, and our children were being educated; the children in the orphanages were also being schooled. But a new superintendent of education joined the diabolic commissar, Isahag Nouri by name, a man who had been educated in the American college of Aintab and had recently fled from there. By his orders all our schools were closed and teaching in the orphanage was forbidden. The former freedom in distributing relief was curtailed.

Through the Near East Relief the Armenians of Marash used to correspond with their loved ones in other places. Now the government began a strict censorship of all Near East Relief mail and no Armenian dared write a letter. For eight months I was unable to get in touch with my son Albert in the American college of Tarsus. All letters sent to Marash from outside were seized; those to whom they were addressed were imprisoned; and only after much suffering and expenditure of money were they able to go free. Even people whose names were mentioned in a letter sent to another ("Remember me to so and so") were arrested.

Mr. McAfee of Beirut, a high official of the Near East Relief, and Mr. Christianson, another official, were arrested while on their way to Marash and thrown into prison. Repeated appeals to Mustafa Kemal were necessary before they were set free. A number of new missionaries and relief workers who wanted to come to Marash were kept waiting for months in Aintab and only after many difficulties were permitted to enter the city. One of the members of the relief, Mr. Kerr, was summoned to court because of the accusation "He helps to send the letters of the Armenians." After a long trial he was declared innocent.

One day all the foreign buildings were surrounded by officials, soldiers, and police. There was a careful search of every cranny and nook. The few rooms I occupied with my family in one of these buildings were also searched. The very closet from which an hour or so before I had removed my writings and my money to a safe place was ransacked. I praised the Lord that they had not been discovered, since my money would have been taken and I would have been arrested because of my writings and cast into prison.

Some American buildings where hundreds of Armenians were living were occupied and all the occupants driven out into the streets. Then the buildings were turned over to Turkish officials.

Sickness and disease began to spread and brought death to many Armenians. The dead, under guard of the gendarmes, were taken without any ceremony and thrown into a ditch.

The trial of the members of the National Union was still going on under the threat of a death sentence. As I have mentioned, a number of the members were already in prison. I was indeed fortunate to be one of those still at liberty.

It was under such terrible pressure, privations, fears, threats, that the Armenian remnant, having barely escaped massacre, was living. And all these things were being done for revenge—because of the defeat suffered by the Turkish forces in Aintab, and because of the free activities of the Armenians in Adana.

One day the Gregorian priest, Khachadoor Vartabed Der Ghazarian, and I were taken to the government building, where a roomful of civil and military officials presented a document to us, signed by all of them, and ordered us to sign also. The document read: "We, the undersigned, agree that all the Americans —missionaries and members of the Relief—must be expelled from Marash. All our misfortunes have their source in such foreigners who, under the guise of religion and benevolence, have come here to sow hatred and tumult in our land. All our calamities issue from them. We ourselves will care for our orphans and people. All Americans, without exception, are political tools. We do not desire their service. They have no usefulness here."

Our signatures were of course the most important of all. Had we signed, they would have had the perfect pretext to drive all the Americans out of the city. What the outcome would be was clear. Once the foreigners were out, all their remaining buildings would be occupied by the Turks. Our fifteen hundred orphans would be in their hands, either to be brought up as Turks or to be used in various cruel ways in their houses and harems. Relief would cease, and our wives and daughters would be forced to beg from lecherous hands, and to become servants of their caprice. To sign this paper was to approve of these consequences and to betray our nation. Yet not to sign meant to incur the wrath and vengeance of these bloodthirsty officials. But no matter what, the leaders of a nation must protect their people, at the risk of their own lives.

Khachadoor Vartabed Der Ghazarian and I did not hesitate in our decision: "We cannot sign a paper of this nature."

What? An answer like this! at a time like this! and in a place such as this! All eyes were fiercely turned on us. We were in the presence of frenzied wolves. We were in a den of lions. But God closed their mouths and they were unable to tear us to pieces. Even so, they kept in their hearts our revolt and boldness.

The pressure on the Armenians was growing daily. We, as the leaders of the people, were forced to take a great part of the relief money given to them for their bread and hand it over to the commissar to pay for his buildings. He of course kept a good part of the money for himself.

The time came when the people were no longer able to endure their burdens and appealed to their leaders for action. In June we called a meeting and decided to petition the mutessarif, pleading that he order the commissar to cease torturing the people. We presented a petition, signed by the three religious heads of the city—Khachadoor Vartabed Der Ghazarian, Kerabaydzar Avedis Arpiarian, and myself.

Next day, very early in the morning, the police came and took me, and Der Sahag and Der Khoren, the representatives of the other two signatories of the petition, to the quarters of the commissar. We knew that some terrible punishment had been planned for us. When the commissar entered the room, he did not greet us. He ordered the police and all others except a *yüzbaşï* to get out. Then he closed the door. Now the commissar, the *yüzbaşï*, and we three Armenians were alone.

"Is this your petition? Are these your signatures?" growled the commissar.

"Yes," we answered.

He began to fume, to blow, to kindle, to flame! He was sizzling, crackling! He began to shout and curse us, our religion, our nation! Like a mad dog he raged, "You are slaves! Our tools! You have no freedom! You have no right! No right to open your mouths! No right to live! You are dogs! Asses! Swine! And even lower than these beasts!"

My friends were older than I and more experienced. They trembled and remained silent. But I was not able to take all this, so I said, "Sir, we are the religious heads of our nation. We have been recognized by the government, and are permitted to protect the rights of our people. We have presented our complaints to the higher authority of the mutessarif and have requested the mercy of the government. You ought not to deal with us in this way, here in this place of justice."

At my words this Satan became a thing hell could not contain. He was mad! Out of himself! He leaped from his chair and came toward me. I did not realize that he was about to blind me.

I was watching him. Suddenly he raised his fist and let it come down on my right eye with all his savagery and strength, holding his thumb like a sharp pick between his fingers. The blow was so terrible that for a moment everything went black. A streak of light flashed before my eyes. Then from my eye and nose blood gushed forth on the floor.

I was silent, biting back my cry of pain. He was getting ready to strike my left eye, but now the *yüzbaşï* came to my rescue and prevented him. The commissar sat down again and continued cursing. Then he added, like the Pharaoh, "Each week from now on you will pay regularly a sum of money twice the amount previously decided upon. And the people will work unceasingly till the buildings are completed!"

In fear of losing my other eye, I did not say a word. Receiving permission, we bowed low, went out, and returned home. I was in bed for two weeks, in great fear that I had lost my eye, but praise be to God, my light had not been darkened. However, for months my eye was black and swollen.

Why had the commissar acted in this way?

When the mutessarif received our petition, he called the commissar to him and ordered him to do exactly what he did to us, so that never again would we consider ourselves free or subject to justice, and that we would do whatever we were told to without complaint.

After this incident, one day, as I was conversing with a Turkish official, he said to me, "My friend, there is no hope. No longer can the Turk and the Armenian live together. Whenever you find the opportunity, you will annihilate us; and whenever we find the opportunity, we will annihilate you. Now the opportunity is ours and we will do everything to harm you. The wise course for you will be, when the time comes, to leave this country and never to return."

This Turk had spoken the truth. No longer could the Turk be a friend to the Armenian, or the Armenian a friend to the Turk.

One day the Gregorian priest, Der Sahag Der Bedrossian and I went to a mosque frequented by the greatest and most influential *hoca* of the city, Dayï Zade *Hoca* by name. The Turks recognized this man as a prophet, and his words were as divine oracles to the people. Because of him even Armenian children had been slaughtered in the courtyard of *Ooloo Jami*. We had come to arouse his pity for the Armenians and to beg him to speak a good word for us so that the Turks would treat us something like human beings.

As we entered the courtyard of the mosque, we saw him sitting in his place surrounded by other *hocalar*, all kneeling before him. Seeing that we wore shoes, he ordered us to take them off. We removed our shoes, approached him humbly, and knelt before him. Immediately he started to talk, shouting that the Armenians were rebels, unfaithful people, and therefore deserved the evils which had befallen them. We did not speak. He turned the monologue to religion. He praised Mohammedanism and tried to show us the errors of Christianity. He wanted us to agree that the inferiority of our religion was obvious. We had gone to awaken his sympathy and to beseech help for our wretched people; he was trying to make us trample upon our own religion.

Der Sahag kept silent, but I was not able to endure this disrespect to my faith. I said, "My Lord, Hoca Effendi, you know that religion is a matter of conscience, a matter of personal relationship between an individual and his Creator. Of course for Moslems, the Mohammedan religion is honorable; and for Christians, the Christian religion."

My bold answer and my apparent defense of Christianity wounded his self-respect. I, a giavoor, a slave! Who was I to express myself before this prophet of Allah! Infuriated, he shouted at us threateningly. The courtyard of the mosque was full of *çete* and soldiers. Only a wave of the hand, and we would have been torn to bits. And just at this delicate moment, the notifications proclaiming the daily events, had arrived, and it was being announced, "In Adana the Armenians are doing such and such evils against the Turks; are murdering them, and are occupying their houses!" What a terrible situation! We were glad that our hoca at this point stood up to go home. All his company immediately arose. We too arose, quickly put on our shoes, and followed him, in great fear that we would be shot from behind.

Der Sahag, of course, had been more polite and humble

whereas my behavior and the few words I had uttered showed me impudent and insolent. As we were coming out of the door of the mosque, the hoca turned to the priest and said, "Whenever you wish you may come to me for an interview." But to me he said, "Never again see my face!"

I had indeed become the object of this man's loathing. Terrified, as I walked toward my house, I said in my mind to my Heavenly Father, "Lord, Pharaoh too said to Moses, 'See my face never again,' and you did not let him see it. You are able to grant this grace to me also, thy other servant. Let me not see his face again."

Of course as soon as this instrument of the devil reached home, he began to think of ways to punish me. But God did not give him an opportunity. After entering his house this day, he never came out again. He developed a fever, and soon after, the solemn voices of the muezzins, coming from the minarets, gave me the glad tidings that the hoca was dead:

> *Allah ekber, Allah ekber.*
> *La ilaha ill-Allah.*
> *Muhammedin Rasula-llah.*

In truth I never saw his face again.

Just around this time the evil commissar also was removed from office and sent back to Angora. One day he spilled his poison on the wrong person, a gendarme who had powerful sponsors. They rose up against the commissar, complained to Angora, and had him transferred. Now two of my worst enemies were no more. But many remained.

During these years another heartrending scene for the Armenians was the indescribable wretchedness of the Greek deportees. Because Greece had occupied Smyrna, the Turks had laid hands on all the Greeks in the empire and under the guise of deportation were killing them off. Just like the Armenians, thousands and thousands of Greeks were driven from their houses, many were massacred on the roads leading to the deserts, their wives and daughters were raped, and the remnant, hun-

166

gry, thirsty, naked, filthy, utterly exhausted, and turned to skeletons, had been scattered here and there in the Turkish villages and cities. Contagious diseases took away hundreds every day. Although we were helping those who had been brought to Marash, nevertheless our help was nothing. To our woes, the woes of these co-Christians were added. Eventually all were taken away and killed.

Still trusting in the Lord, I was trying to perform all my duties faithfully, even to the bitter end, by keeping the people alive with the relief, and also by offering them spiritual consolation.

As I have mentioned, the Aintab war had ended and the Turkish Army, with more than ten thousand troops, was ready under the generalship of Salahaddin Pasha. Hadjin had been razed to the ground; the Armenians there were no more. The Marash Armenians were in the chains of slavery. Nothing remained but to destroy brave little Zeytoon.

The majority of the approximately one thousand Zeytoontsis were widows, children, and old folks. There were hardly three hundred who were able to fight. All the people lived quietly in the barracks. There was no revolutionary movement whatever. They were living at peace with their neighboring Turks. Their leader, Aram Bey, was shepherding them well. But in the eyes of the Turk a handful of Zeytoontsis, living freely on the summit of a mountain, and in his own barracks, and especially the presence of his bitter enemy, Aram Bey, who many times had slashed at his pride—this was not an endurable thing. The Turk knows how to keep mum, to bide his time, to design, to wait. He is a politician. He knows the circumstances, the right occasion. He can dampen the fire of his revenge and then let it blaze out against his enemies at the opportune moment.

The military and civil officials of Marash and all the Armenian-hating aghas had met and decided to despoil Zeytoon and to scatter the Zeytoontsis. One day we Armenian religious leaders were summoned. "The Zeytoontsis must give up all their guns," we were told. "After that, if they choose, they may live in Zeytoon; if not they may move to Marash and live with the Armenians of Marash."

What was our opinion? Of course we could not have disagreed with them, so we said, "Very well, since you have decided thus, the Zeytoontsis must obey."

We were asked to send letters to Zeytoon and to invite a few delegates to Marash to arrange this matter with them. We agreed. Letters were written and sent.

A few days later three Zeytoontsis came to Marash. Again a meeting was called. Salahaddin Pasha told the delegates what he had to say. The poor delegates tried in vain to persuade him that they had no guns, that they were living at peace and in obedience and would continue so to live.

The meeting dispersed, and the delegates from Zeytoon were put on their way under the guard of gendarmes. At the same time three thousand soldiers also started out. Their purpose was to conquer Zeytoon. Already the order had been given to the Turkish and Cherkess villagers to cut off Zeytoon from every side so that no one might escape.

It was the month of July—the month of Zeytoon's second massacre and deportation. The army had reached Zeytoon, the cannons had been entrenched at vantage points all around, machine guns were ready to fire. The delegates entered the barracks and gave the Zeytoontsis this unexpected and calamitous news. The Turkish general had sent an ultimatum to Aram Bey to surrender unconditionally in two hours and to allow the troops to enter the barracks without any resistance; otherwise the firing would begin.

What were these unhappy people going to do? There was no time to think, to organize, to decide. Aram Bey, who in 1915 had battled the Turks and been victorious; who in the same year had taken part in the conflict of Fundejak and, after overthrowing many Turks, escaped; who for three years had remained on Giavoor Dagh with his Braves; who only recently had saved his thousand Zeytoontsis from slaughter—in this terrible time also he kept his courage and balance of mind, and did the possible best. He immediately ordered all women, children, girls, the old, the weak, and even the young men who so desired, to go out and surrender to the army. Wailing, in tears and in woe, these people left the barracks and surrendered to the army. The general examined them one by one. Those who had fathers or husbands still in the barracks were sent back with the words "Either you come together with your men or you will be killed with them."

Thus about six hundred were kept with the soldiers and finally put on the road toward Marash. The other four hundred, two hundred of them able to bear arms—the rest being children and women—remained in the barracks, and shells and bullets began to fly. The battle lasted for twelve hours, until midnight that day. The three thousand troops did not dare to enter the barracks. The Zeytoon Braves, under the leadership of Aram Bey, fought against the enemy on one side, to prevent their entrance, and on the other, they led the people away in the darkness, through difficult paths, up the mountains, taking with them a little food and leaving behind about fifty of the sick and weak.

The firing from the barracks ceased. The soldiers entered to find these enfeebled fifty and, in partial revenge, mercilessly massacred all of them. Under the orders of the general, these three thousand troops and the Turkish riffraff then climbed the mountains to hunt down their escaped victims on every side.

The six hundred Zeytoontsis entered Marash on the third day of the attack, in a most wretched condition. Permission was given to the Americans to help them, and they were brought to the courtyard of one of the American buildings, where they sat in the open, in the dirt and dust. A sad scene! The former scenes were being repeated. My mind and body were no longer able to bear them. I was on the verge of a stroke. All the Armenians of Marash were one with me in lamentation. The Turks were happy because now this thorn in their flesh—the eternal cause of their grief—finally had been pulled out.

The Near East Relief officials did their very best to feed these people and to keep them alive; and that cunning and sly Salahaddin Pasha, the murderer of Hadjin and Zeytoon, began to send daily provisions, so that in a few weeks the Zeytoontsis were in plenty!

But what of the Braves who had rebelled on the mountain? Like eagles they were fleeing from valley to valley and from mountain to mountain, hiding from the rage of their hunters.

Whenever the enemy came near, they would open fire on them, and during these encounters their women, children, the old, and the weak fell and were left alone to die of hunger and thirst or be shot by the enemy. In this way their numbers decreased from day to day, and soon only the Braves were left. This unbearable condition lasted almost a month; how many times they fought the Turks face to face and drove them back! And it was in one of these fate-in-hand battles that our fearless Aram Bey received the bullet of an enemy and fell lifeless to the ground, leaving his faithful friends in despair.

Now the rest of the Zeytoontsis began to seek a way to descend the mountains and if possible reach either Adana or Aintab. But what a difficult undertaking! They could travel only at night, and through dangerous paths! They had nothing to eat. Every place was full of murderers who had been ordered to shoot down these fugitives wherever they were found.

One day they set out. They traveled for a few days on the road to Adana but were espied by the Turks and fiercely attacked. Some were killed. Some were taken captive. The rest, in retreat, retraced their footsteps for days and found themselves again on their beloved mountain.

After holding out on the mountain for a few weeks, they made another attempt to flee, this time toward Aintab. After many hardships and losses, some finally did reach Aintab, went over to the French, and were saved. The greater part, led by Hovhannes Simonyan, one of Aram Bey's officers, almost reached Aleppo but were met by another Turkish attack. They fought. They killed and were killed. Simonyan fell, but about fifty Braves managed to enter Aleppo and were saved. Of the four hundred, hardly one hundred and fifty persons escaped in this or that way —after unimaginable privations and most miraculously.

The Turks were now happy and fearless. Zeytoon was no more. Its name was now *Suleimaniya*, and Turks were living there. The six hundred Zeytoontsis in Marash had to be kept out of sight of the Turks lest their presence offend them! Perhaps these women, old folks, and children might some day rise up and massacre the Turks!

We in Marash were now convinced that our very existence

Courtesy of Stanley E. Kerr

Deportees Returning to Marash

Aram Bey, One of the Cholakian Brothers

Courtesy of the Hartunian Family

The Hartunian Family in 1920

Courtesy of Armenian Democratic Liberal Organization

Talaat Pasha

Orphans near Death from Starvation

Orphans Being Cared For

Courtesy of Armenian Democratic Liberal Organization

Smyrna After the Fire

Courtesy of Armenian Democratic Liberal Organization

Refugees Hoping to Get Aboard Ships at Smyrna

was in great danger. The young men, surfeited by the heavy yoke of "military service," exhausted by their daily hard and unpaid for labors, terrified by the horrors of the future, and encouraged by the news that finally some of the Zeytoontsis had reached Aintab and Aleppo, began, in groups of ten, twenty, or even more, to escape in the night. The first few attempts were successful because as yet they were secret, and the government had no knowledge of them. Thus many reached Aintab safely. Some even succeeded in reaching Adana. But when the government found out about this exodus, it took severe measures. The easiest thing to do was to put pressure on the religious heads.

Wednesday, August 10, was my forty-ninth birthday. A dinner was given in my honor by the missionaries and the members of the Near East Relief in a garden near the city. These friends knew my cares, my burdens, my work, and they desired at least this day to make me forget them. Did I not have the right to enjoy life at least one day in the year? Apparently not. Suddenly a gendarme came up to me, and taking me from my friends, my wife and children, he led me to the *konak*, where I found the other two religious leaders, Der Ghazarian and Avedis Arpiarian. An accusation had been prepared which would send us to a higher authority to be imprisoned. What had we done? We had advised, encouraged, and persuaded the young men of the city to escape to Aintab and to Adana!

"We did no such thing. We know nothing about this." But these were vain words here.

"You are going to prison!"

We used all our talents. We knew that once we entered prison there was no coming out. Our poor friends—the members of the Union—and other Armenians, about forty in all, were still in prison after two years.

We soon discovered that the accusation was something brewed up by this gendarme and one official; the higher officials had not yet entered the plot. We three religious heads consulted together and decided to buy our freedom if possible. And sure enough, promised a certain sum, the official and the gendarme tore up the accusation and threw it into the fire. We were free.

It was very late when I reached the garden again. My loved

ones and my friends were in great anxiety. I ate my food. I received my gifts. Only one day in the year—and that too was mixed in its happiness and pain.

As I have mentioned, the Turks used to receive messages from Adana to the effect that the Armenians were treating them most cruelly there. In revenge, they would molest us in Marash. Our suffering gave them pleasure. They thought up new, unheard-of ways to frighten us and to oppress us. Now they had found something very new indeed! An Armenian girl of about twelve years had been deported from one of the cities of Anadoloo and abandoned in these parts. Abducted by a Turk in one of the villages near Aintab, she had been forced to become his wife, but three years of daily beatings by her husband was more than she could bear and she had run away. One day, traveling toward Aintab, she was arrested by a gendarme. Though during the cross-examination the truth about her came out, she was brought to Marash and forced by beatings and threats to say that she was a spy, that she went back and forth between Marash and Aintab carrying letters between the Armenians of Marash and the French of Aintab.

This girl was dressed up as a boy and paraded through the streets of the city. The Turkish people were delighted by this sport—"An Armenian spy has been arrested!"—and we were assailed by new fears, and with us the six hundred Zeytoontsis. Now a perfect pretext had been invented to arrest Armenians, to imprison them, torture them, kill them. The "revenge" of the Turk has neither measure nor limit.

The officials gave this supposed spy a list of names to learn, then brought the people named before her and asked, "Do you recognize this man? Did this man give you any letters?" And the poor girl, conditioned by the whip, was forced to say "Yes!"

The first blow fell on an innocent Armenian priest, Der Movses Kahana by name. He was arrested and imprisoned. The same night he was bastinadoed one hundred and fifty times so that he would confess that he had given letters to the spy and that other Armenians were involved in espionage. Weak in body but powerful in spirit, this priest insisted that the accusation was false and that no Armenian was in any way involved. Only after he had fainted did the beating cease. The poor man was held in the Turkish prison for four months.

Now all the Armenians of Marash were awaiting their turn. Others were successively arrested under the same accusation and in the same way beaten and thrown into prison, next to our brave and upright priest.

One day a policeman came and directed me to the *konak*. An Armenian layman was also there. A little later the investigating body of the court-martial entered, bringing the spy with them. My turn had come. Did the spy recognize me? What a critical and decisive moment! The girl answered, "No, I do not recognize him."

What had happened?

The question was repeated, "Don't you recognize this man?"

"No!" said the girl again.

"Do you recognize him?" asked the examiner, pointing to the layman.

"I don't recognize either one of them," answered the spy. She was sent away. We were free.

Why did the girl act this way? I do not know. Who knows how she was beaten, how she suffered for speaking as she did! Who knows if afterwards, under the agony of the blows, she herself did not regret her action and ask, "Why did I not say I knew them?"

While, on the one hand, this new invention kept the Armenian people in constant fear and trembling, on the other hand, preparations were being made to deport the six hundred Zeytoontsis along with the notable Armenian families of Marash. The last week of August and the first week of September had been set aside to get this plan under way. By now Salahaddin Pasha had gone, and a military man bearing an accursed name had succeeded him, Talaat Bey. Mustafa Remzi Pasha had also left and been replaced by Shefket Bey, the exact negative of his name for he possessed not a dram of pity. The commissar at this time was a venal, lewd man. There was not a single person in the government from whom we could expect any good. All the malefactors of earth, it seemed, had united to bring all possible evil against the Armenians.

One day I was taken into the presence of the governor. Talaat Bey was there too. "We are concerned about the deported Zeytoontsis," they said to me, "lying unsheltered in the courtyard in the dust and dirt. We have therefore appropriated a good building for them. Gather all of them there and let them be comfortably sheltered."

I believed them. I expressed my thanks and immediately undertook this task. I had the building cleaned and made ready —and in truth it was a good, large building—and in a few days the Zeytoontsis were settled and happy.

Hardly had they rested one day when the building was surrounded by gendarmes. A list was made of all the names, and two days later the wretched people were sent off toward Chermoug, one of the cities of the vilayet of Diyarbekir. Whatever they had brought with them from Zeytoon was later confiscated by the Turks. Among these people were two very old priests and also that Lion of Furnus, Partoghomios Vartabed, who in 1895, during the struggle of Zeytoon, had frowned on the Turkish captive soldiers passing beneath his sword. Now he was old and weak and could be driven along easily by ordinary gendarmes. All the Zeytoontsis, even the women and children, were walking, many barefooted, to the joy of the Turks and to the misery of the Armenians. This night for the first time the Turks were sleeping undisturbed. And my mind was grinding horrors as I thought of the part I had played in this subtle plan. I had been asked to congregate these Zeytoontsis in one building, so that they should all be in one place, easily rounded up and taken away without the trouble of looking for those who might otherwise have hidden in their friends' houses.

A Turkish official told me, "You and a good number of others were going to be sent too, but it was prevented somehow."

The spy game was still being played. Hardly six weeks after my first escape from the trap a summons came: "*Casusluk maddesinden dolayï teftişat için Divan-i Harb'a geliniz.* Appear at Court-Martial for investigation in the espionage case." All the other religious heads of the city and all the Armenian notables had also been summoned.

The day set for the investigation arrived. I, two other religious heads, and the layman who was with me at the first investigation, appeared first at court. We had a servant with us also who, holding our canes, was standing next to us. The spacious room and yard of the courthouse were full of soldiers, Turkish common people, and military and civil officials. Clearly the Turks had no other amusement. Just as a cat enjoys torturing a mouse, so these Turks were enjoying torturing us.

A *binbaşi* was the justice of the court-martial, and we the accused were humbly standing before him in the following order: the Catholic priest, the Gregorian priest, myself, and the layman. The spy was next to the *binbaşi*.

The *binbaşi* directed his words to the spy: "Boy, spy, look! This is the Catholic priest, Kerabaydzar; this is the Gregorian priest, Der Ghazarian; this is the Protestant Badveli; and that man is Dajat Dakesian. Which one of these do you recognize?"

The spy immediately shouted, "I recognize the Protestant Badveli."

Of course until this poor girl had learned to say this, she had suffered many beatings.

Thus the first investigation was over, and the *binbaşi* retired to his room with the spy. Now she had to be instructed to say she recognized all the rest.

Sitting near me was a military officer with whom I was somewhat friendly. While the *binbaşi* and the spy were in their private room, this man got up and, taking me out of line, made me stand next to the wall. Now the other two religious heads were standing on one side, Dajat, the layman, next to them, and our servant next to Dajat. Soon the *binbaşi* came out with the spy and again said, "Do you recognize these?" The girl at first had seen four persons and she still saw four persons. I was somewhat apart, and she, not noticing the change, said, "Yes, I recognize all four. These two priests, and the man next to them, and that man next to him who is holding the canes."

This time the Badveli was not recognized! Names had always been given to the girl, and there were explanations and descriptions. But she was unable to keep them in her mind, so the artificial and deliberately planned form of these accusations was clear to all.

Our poor servant began to tremble. "I'm not one of these four," he said. "I'm their servant. Where do you know me from?" Now all those present, even the *binbaşi*, began to laugh because of this ridiculous, base, deceitful proceeding. But it was enough that the mouse was being tortured in the claws of the cat and that the cat was being amused.

This part over, we were locked in a room and called out one by one to be cross-examined. All the questions revolved around political crimes. Our answers were recorded and we were made to sign them. After the cross-examinations the *binbaşi* told us, "According to law it is necessary that all of you be imprisoned, even your servant. But for the present I will set you free. You will be summoned again in the near future."

We expressed our thanks and departed. Fifteen others were subjected to the same ordeal and like us were released to be summoned again later on.

Now I was regarded as a political culprit by two courts, and I was always being prosecuted by them. Every day I was under the fear of imprisonment. In the Criminal Court or the Supreme Court my friends and I were accused of being the cause of the war of Marash. In the court-martial I was accused of corresponding with the French with the intent to bring the French forces back to Marash. These were two great crimes, punishable, according to Turkish law, by death.

But there were three courts in the city, and it was necessary that I be incriminated by the third. The Criminal Court and the court-martial had done their duty. Now the Magistrates Court, under another pretext, must brand me a political offender. This court too soon found what it was looking for.

After the massacre of 1920 the government confiscated the remaining houses, vineyards, and fields of the dead and fugitive Armenians. But those who were still alive and in Marash could, supposedly, repossess their properties and sell them if they chose. We religious heads, to verify such claims, used to give certificatory notes to the Armenians, and the government, depending on these, seemingly went through certain official proceedings. I had given a great many such certificates and now was being accused of falsifying one of them. I had said that the husband of a certain woman was alive (the man *was* still alive at the time of this accusation). But the court had "established" his death, and there was no question now as to truth or falsity. It was enough that the accusation incriminated me.

These three courts became the offices of my daily business. One day I was taken here; another day, there. I was always cross-examined and threatened with imprisonment and death.

Thus through such heavy and nerve-wracking circumstances, I reached the last months of the year. Then one day a proclamation was made: "The Turks and the French have come to an agreement. Everything is well. The Armenians at last are free and safe."

We simple-minded Armenians were again happy and hopeful. We breathed deeply. We thought the gain of foreigners was ours. But two days later this deceptive happiness vanished. We learned what the terms of the agreement were and what they signified for us. All of Cilicia—Adana, Aintab, Marash, Kilis— was to be left to the Turks. The French were about to withdraw from these places. Again, woe was our lot.

Before long difficulties arose in Adana. The Armenians said to the French, "You have no right to leave us!" And the French answered, "We have orders to leave!"

Now the Armenians began to leave Adana, Aintab, Kilis—all of Cilicia. It was announced in Marash too: "Those who wish to leave may do so. Passports will be given to them."

When I heard this announcement, my first act was to persuade all my people to quickly depart from the city. And group after group appealed to the government for their passports. The first three groups were put safely on their way and reached Aleppo. But the fourth, composed of about a thousand people, among whom was the Near East Relief worker Miss Matter, was attacked on the road about four hours' distance from the city. All were robbed and beaten; on foot, in a half-dead condition, they reached Aintab, and from there went on toward Aleppo. Ah, the Turks were grieved that their victims were fleeing. They wanted to hunt them down for the last time, to experience the last pleasure of torturing the helpless. All the booty (bedding, hats, shoes, clothes, cooking utensils, some money—whatever these poor people had been able to save during the last two years by the help of the relief) was brought to Marash, and the aghas and officials who had planned the attack divided it among themselves.

The same day another small group set out to join this larger one, about fifteen persons who had been a little late starting. A Turkish detachment assaulted them and after a number of pretty girls were cruelly raped, they and the small children and all the old folk were massacred. Yet despite all these things the government did nothing.

The missionaries and the members of the relief, because one of their workers had been attacked and robbed, used this fact to protest to Angora on behalf of the Armenians, and an order was issued by wire not to repeat such things. But who knows what the secret orders were?

The year was nearing its end. Of ten thousand Armenians, three thousand had emigrated.

On December 25, Christmas Sunday, I felt I too should look to my preparations to emigrate. Next day I took this matter in prayer to my Lord and submitted it to his guidance: "If thou, O Lord, desirest me to remain here for the consolation of this unhappy remnant, it is well. But if thou desirest that I too depart with my family, lead thou me."

That very day brought a letter from Tarsus, from my son Albert. There were no Armenians left in Adana, Tarsus, and their surroundings, and he too would leave Tarsus on Wednesday, December 28, to go to Mersin, and from there to Smyrna to enter the American International College.

January 4 was the last day decided upon for the withdrawal of the French forces and the occupation of Cilicia by the Turkish forces. On Saturday, December 31, I submitted my petition for a passport and began to get ready.

The year had ended.

12

SUNDAY, JANUARY 1, 1922, I passed with the remnant of my people in spiritual meditation, in hymns, and in prayer. I consoled them and I was consoled. During the following days I was busy getting my passport, making my preparations, and helping my people.

January 15 was an unforgettable Sunday for Marash. Our place of prayer was crowded with a great multitude. The Holy Table of the Lord's Communion was before us with its sublime presence. We all knew that this was the last communion table in Turkey, and especially in our beloved Marash. In a little while all of us would be scattered to the four corners of the world.

Marash was no more. Her magnificent churches, her populous centers, her pure air, her living waters, her beloved friendships, her individual nests, and most precious of all, her evangelical work were no more. Her Gospel to strange peoples was no more. With the commemoration of Christ's death we were also commemorating the death of our nation, her passion, her crucifixion, her burial.

Before this sacred presence I spoke to the people on the victory of Christ's work. And I tried to make them understand that the seeds of truth scattered throughout Turkey for many years, wet with the tears and nourished with the blood of Armenian

179

martyrs, had not perished and would not perish. "Although they sleep, secret and unseen in the depths of the earth, yet they will some day sprout and flower and give fruit. The time will come when all this land will be Christ's."

The administration of the Holy Communion was ended. From every eye teardrops rolled. Our last service had closed.

Farewell Turkey.
Farewell the places where I was born, grew up, and lived.
Farewell my consecrated and holy temples, foundations of wisdom and knowledge—mounds mixed with the ashes of Armenian martyrs and dyed in their blood.
Farewell the unwearied toils of years of mission zeal.
Farewell the magnificence, the fruit of immolation of Armenian religious guides and the labors of Armenian-Christian young men.
Farewell my beloved people and consecrated church and holy flock.
Farewell my twenty-five years of heavy, yet most rewarding preaching, shepherding, and patriotic work.
Farewell thou precious evangelical work. For thee, for thy love, for thy advancement, for thy glory, the Armenian nation lived, suffered, testified, was persecuted, was martyred, and today is laid in the grave. She dies that thou mayest live, and, persuaded that thou livest, she dies happily.
Farewell thou martyr Armenian—universally known, trusting, and faithful. Thou champion of Christianity! Thou forerunner of civilization, magnanimous, brave, the master of moral and spiritual strength. Faithful to principle, to dignity, to value, to morality, who for their love despisest even life itself!
Farewell!
Although the Turk proved himself unjust, although the European showed himself most false, although the American broke faith in selfishness and fear, yet God exists and is, with his justice, holiness, omnipotence, and government. Because he lives, your dead shall come to life. Your fallen shall rise. Your just cause shall overcome. And as the death of Jesus was

the salvation of the individual world, so your death shall be the salvation of the universal world.

Therefore, O Armenians, martyrs scattered to the corners of the world, pilgrim children, be comforted, be encouraged, and wait in patience for the glorious future blessing about to befall the world.

*   *   *

On January 21, 1922, just two years after the Marash war, I received my passport. Next day, Sunday, I performed the sacrament of baptism. I preached on January 29 and again on February 5. The text of my last sermon in Marash was: "If it is not possible that this cup pass from me but that I drink it, let thy will be done."

On Monday, February 6, I had my last session with my official board, and we settled all our old and new accounts. On Wednesday I met with the officials of the Near East Relief. Then I was ready to start out.

I had hired animals and carriages to transport my family and our belongings, but at the last moment some Armenians who had Turkish friends in government circles informed me that my Turkish enemies had organized a band of cutthroats to attack us on the road and kill us. I informed the Near East Relief officials, and Mr. Kerr, the president, kindly offered to help us escape. He had already appealed to the government for permission to go to Aintab in his automobile and to return. The government of Marash had telegraphed to Angora, and this very day, February 8, the permission had reached him. We therefore left our belongings in Marash to be brought later by muleteers, got into Mr. Kerr's automobile about four o'clock in the morning, and in the darkness, secretly, left Marash. In four hours we reached Aintab; our murderers lost their victims.

Two hours after our arrival in Aintab Mr. Kerr came to me holding a telegram in his hand, with the good news that one of the members of the relief, Dr. Wilson, a comrade of my sufferings and at this time in America, had sent me one thousand dollars for my expenses to America.

We passed February 9, 10, and 11 in Aintab, entertained by the Americans and a number of Armenian friends. February 11 was my youngest son's birthday, and now, in semi-freedom, we celebrated it.

On Sunday, February 12, joining a large group that had arrived from Marash the previous day, we set out toward Kilis. On the way, we came to a place called *Kazïklï* where we passed a dangerous hour. For some time it had been raining and snowing, and the waters of a stream we had to cross were swollen. The bridge had been washed away. Our carriages and overloaded donkeys could not carry us across the stream. When the carriages were emptied, the horses were able to pull them across, but we were left on the other side.

Soon some Arab villagers came to us and said, "Give us money and we will take you across."

At first I feared that they were deceiving us, that they would rob us and take away our girls—something they had done to previous groups and did to groups coming after us. But since there was no other way, I agreed to let them help us. Fortunately, what I had feared did not come to pass, we were taken across the stream, and that night we were in Kilis at an inn.

We remained February 13 in Kilis and next day started toward Aleppo. Suddenly gendarmes and officials were all about us, opening our bundles and trunks and searching them. I had a trunk full of books and writings. If these were found, it would mean disaster for me. I would be sent back. There would be long-drawn-out investigations. I knew the psychology of the Turks. Calling the head official to me while the possessions of others were being searched, I gave him a gold piece.

"*Bïrak git, efendi!* Go on, sir!" he said, meaning I could proceed without being searched.

We drove on and crossed the Turkish frontier. In another hour we saw a French flag waving over a village. Although this was the flag under which we had been so persecuted, it was a hair more encouraging than the Turkish flag.

This day we reached Aleppo, where we stayed from February 14 until May 3. During this time I tried to get my passport for America but met constant difficulties because of my eyes

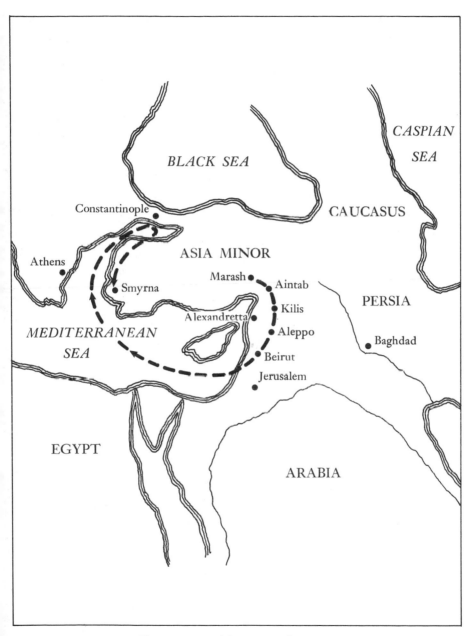

ESCAPE FROM MARASH TO SMYRNA

and my wife's eyes. Nevertheless, our days here passed more peacefully and enjoyably.

Several letters arrived from my son in Smyrna, and I was happy that he too was well and safe.

Marash now was already empty of Armenians. They had congregated in Aleppo, and most of them were living in tents.

On April 20 I received an invitation from Smyrna to work there as a pastor. And because I had not been able to get a passport to America from here, and because my son was in Smyrna, and because Smyrna was, after all, on the way to America, I thought it proper to accept this invitation and make my last decision for the future there. Thus writing to Smyrna that I was ready to come, I immediately set out to procure a passport for Smyrna.

On April 26 my passport was issued, but one of the officials of the relief informed me that the thousand dollars for my traveling expenses had been sent back to Dr. Wilson. This money could not be kept for more than three months; if the traveler did not set out for America within that time, it had to be returned to its sender until some new arrangements were made. Of course this news was disheartening. But, persuaded that in it there was also a providential secret and good, I said, "Let God's will be done."

When I told the American consul, Mr. Jackson, that I was going to Smyrna, he seemed to regret that he had to visa my passport. He tried to put off the visaing, saying that I should take my passport for Smyrna to the French official and have added to it *New York*—that is, to Smyrna and from Smyrna to New York. With his recommendation, the French official changed the passport in this way. Next Mr. Jackson gave me a good recommendation directed to Mr. George Horton, the American consul in Smyrna, asking him, when the time came, to visa my passport for America.

My work thus arranged, on Thursday, May 4, we left Aleppo by train, reached Beirut about midnight, and were received by my former friend, Mr. Nishan Salibian, who had been a member of my church in Marash and a few years previously had moved here.

In Beirut I had my passport visaed for Smyrna by the Greek consul. On Tuesday, May 9, just three months after leaving Marash, we sailed from Beirut on the French steamship *Lamartine.* After a delightful calm voyage we anchored before Constantinople on Saturday, May 13. And on Sunday, May 14, six years after my first Sunday in Baghtche, we were in Smyrna.

13

Surrounded by many friends, and reunited with our son, who had been away from us for three years, we were exceedingly happy. In a few days we became acquainted with the Evangelical community and with the missionaries and soon joined together with a strong tie of friendship.

The church invited me to serve her for two years. I saw that the city was very pleasant. Safety and peace prevailed under the government and protection of Greece. There were good schools for our children. The Turks and Christians were very friendly toward each other. Business was brisk, and the people were enjoying life. No clouds appeared on the face of heaven. I therefore accepted this invitation and began my work. The church quickly became organized. I listed one hundred and fifty families, totaling about five hundred people.

This year the annual conference of the Bithinian Armenian Evangelical Union was to be held in Constantinople. I was invited to attend and reached Constantinople on July 3. The session of the conference continued from Wednesday the fifth until Monday the tenth. Important matters were discussed. Fine decisions were made. Inspired services were held. We returned to our cities full of joy.

On Sunday, July 16, autonomy was declared for Smyrna and

its surroundings. The day was celebrated majestically, with color-
ful, gay parades. The common people—both Greek and Armenian communities—considered it a day of salvation. But for those
who understood the cause of this declaration, for the Christians
of Smyrna and its environs, it was the foreteller of woes and sufferings to come. I said to one of my friends, "This is a day of
evil for us. Remember my words."

I now regretted that I had remained here rather than immediately continuing on to America. But I had let the opportunity slip. Now I had to submit to my destiny. I had passed through
six terrible massacres. It was necessary to count the seventh.

Days and weeks went by. Outwardly there was nothing to
cause discouragement. But the inner and secret rottenness had
begun.

On Sunday, August 6, a great mass meeting was held in honor
of England and her Prime Minister, Lloyd George. Now was the
time, with outward shows, to fool the trusting people! Lloyd
George had delivered a powerful address in Parliament for the
benefit of the Greeks. The speech, the speaker, and Britain were
being praised to high heaven. What magnificent parades marched
down the streets! Flags! British, Greek, and, among others, Armenian flags, waving side by side! Before the British consulate
speeches were being delivered and hurrahs shouted. The whole
day had been dedicated to this purpose. Once again fooled, and
ignorant of coming disaster, the poor people withdrew happily
to their houses. But not those Christians who saw the inner side
of it all.

Less than two weeks after this meeting the ill news reached
us. On Friday, August 25, the Afion Kara-Hissar frontier had
been shattered by the Turks. The Greek Army was in retreat.
From the surrounding cities and villages the wretched Christians,
leaving behind all their belongings, were fleeing toward Smyrna.
Slowly the wagons of wounded Greeks passed through the streets
of the city. Everywhere were crowds of retreating soldiers. No
longer was there any secret. The Christians of Smyrna had
been betrayed!

The wife and children of the long-deceased and much beloved former pastor of Smyrna, Rev. Hagop Tashjian, who were

then living in America, had expressed their desire to have a new gravestone placed over his tomb. Much money had been spent and this gravestone was now ready. On Sunday, August 27, the announcements for a service of remembrance were made, and the following day, with great solemnity, it was performed. While we were reviving the memory of one long dead, the glorious celebration of the death and burial of the Christians of Asia Minor—Christians who had only recently escaped from death and were just beginning to live once more—was being planned!

The days to come were cursed days. No Christians were left in the environs of Smyrna or in the regions from where the Greek Army was retreating. They all had poured into Smyrna. The fleeing soldiers and the wounded were being brought to Smyrna and taken to Greece in ships.

With nearly half a million Christians, every church, every institution, every street was filled up. Filth, sickness, hunger, nakedness, hardship were widespread. The price of everything suddenly went up. Famine prevailed. The people would crowd around the bakeries, shouting and pushing, snatching bread from each others' hands. The city had been left unprotected. There was no order or government. Everything but the great betrayal and its consequent evils was secondary. The advance of the Turkish Army terrorized every heart. My God! Surfeited by such terrors, I came here to find peace, and behold, the former evils are here too!

I began to advise the people, "Whoever is able to find a ship and to depart from the city, let him go!"

I began to think too of the safety of my own. On Saturday, September 2, I requested the American consul to grant me a visa for America, and because my son Albert did not have a passport for America, I had to appeal to the Greek officials to get one.

September 3 was my last Sunday in Smyrna. I preached on the same text I had used in Marash on my last Sunday there: "Let thy will be done."

Before the service was over, a Greek priest came into my church. Sensing that he had something important to say to me, I cut my sermon short. The Greek Metropolitan wished to see me. When I arrived the wide courtyard and spacious hall of the cathedral were filled to capacity with people. Fearful and bewildered, the Christian population wanted assurance. After deliberating a while with the Metropolitan, we decided to appeal to the consuls of the foreign powers.

We went and spoke to them, besought protection and safety for the people. But almost without exception they remained cold and unconcerned. The most cold-blooded and disinterested was the British consul. We returned more dejected than before, convinced that the Christian powers had united with the Turks to annihilate the Christians of Asia Minor. We tried to say something encouraging to our people but had no words of that nature.

In terror and hopelessness we felt ourselves tossed to and fro. There was no moral strength left in us. Still we had to work. Day by day there had been fewer and fewer Greek soldiers, police, and officials. We learned that they too were running away.

On Monday, September 4, I was busy trying to get my son's passport but could not complete the innumerable formalities that had to be gone through. We had the last session of my official board—a session of extreme sadness! After much anxiety I received my son's passport on September 6. It was the last passport signed by the Greek officials. I went immediately to the American consul for his visa, and, thinking that a ship for America would not be found easily, then procured a passport for my whole family for Constantinople and had it visaed by the British consul.

That night we had our last prayer meeting in the two churches.

On Thursday, September 7, I went again to the American consulate for final visas and was told to come back the next day. The consulate was busy today. Why? Because they had to put their citizens on shipboard and take them away from the city. All the other consulates were likewise busy removing *their* citizens. But what about the half-million Greeks and Armenians? Children and women? Let them be massacred! Their death sentence has already been given!

Why this conscienceless dealing? European politics and especially French interests required it! Why did not Greece with her ships transport her people, the Greeks? She too had dehumanized herself! The Christians of Smyrna must be destroyed! This was the politics of the twentieth century!

Our heaven was now totally eclipsed. We had no stars. Mind, heart, body had once again lost their balance. Like madmen, we rushed here and there, saying to each other, "That base, murderous, Moslem Turk dealt with us better than these European Christians! If only we had known this before and dealt instead with the Turk!"

But that opportunity had passed. Turk and European jointly had turned against us.

The Turkish Army was now nearing the city. Only fragments of the Greek Army were still about. The Turks of the city were proud. The Christians were defeated. On every side hope had vanished, and the people, wringing their hands, were wandering aimlessly here and there, bewailing their evil fate.

We religious heads again met and this time decided to appeal to the Greek governor, Steighiades, and to the Greek general, Hadgianesti. From both we received the same severe answer: "Who are you to meddle in political affairs? We cannot reveal every secret to you! A soldier never flees! We have Smyrna under guard in every way! Smyrna is safe! There is nothing to fear!"

With these words they mocked at us, deceived us, and sent us away.

Woe unto you, unjust diplomacy! Shameless, ignoble, deceitful diplomacy! The Greek nation deceived her people and betrayed them to the Turk, to be strangled by his hands! I spit on you, hellish diplomacy!

The next morning, September 8, all the Greek officials, among them these two, fled from the city. Not one Greek official! Not one guard! The city had now been left to its fate.

I went to the American consulate. The building was being emptied, and books and documents were being packed. The consul visaed my passport (the last one he did), and somewhat relieved, I returned home.

When we saw that again we had been betrayed, we religious heads decided to appeal to the Turkish notables and, if it were possible, come to an agreement with them and so preserve the peace of the city. They received us with more courtesy than the Christian consuls and Greek officials. We then went in a body to the consuls to request them to take over the government of the city. The British consul, in the presence of all, reprimanded the Greek Metropolitan Chrysostomos, that holy, aged man, saying, "You Greeks are the cause of all this evil!" This was the same consul to whom all the people of Smyrna, including the Metropolitan, a few weeks previously had proffered great ceremonial praises. This man did more than just shift the blame. He placed his hand on the shoulder of one of the Turkish notables, and smiling said to him and to all the Turks there, "Don't be afraid! There is nothing. Feel assured."

Next we went to the American consulate, where we found the French consul too. When we presented our case, the latter said hypocritically, "There is no danger for the city. The necessary precautions have been taken." But the saddest man was the American consul, Mr. George Horton. He said nothing, but his expression revealed his mind: "Wretched Christians! European greed, jealousy, competition, and twentieth-century politics sacrifice you in cunning piety! I regret that America too has a silent part and says nothing because of oil interests!"

More than ever dejected, we returned to our places. I had hoped to sail today to Constantinople with my family but had not been successful in finding passage. Nevertheless, many had been able to leave the city and thus would escape the coming terrible events, for which I was glad.

On Saturday morning, September 9, the long quay of Smyrna was crowded from one end to the other with frantic people. Everyone wanted to board a ship and sail away. But there was no ship and no one to take them away.

The Turks, guns in their hands, were prowling happily through the streets. Now and then they would set an Armenian or a Greek house on fire. With anxious joy they were awaiting the entrance of the Turkish Army. The Armenians and the Greeks, hopeless and abandoned, were waiting for their death.

Hurrying toward the quay I saw some of the officials of the steamship line and reserved places in a ship scheduled to leave for America on Tuesday, September 12. I had hopes that the Turkish Army would not occupy the city before then.

On my return home, I saw the leader of the Armenians, Der Khevont Tourian. He took me into his carriage, and we undertook to interview the Turkish aghas once more. But now from every side bullets flew. It was impossible to go by the usual road. Therefore we took a longer and more roundabout route and reached the outskirts of the Turkish quarters. We could go no farther. In front of us a corpse was stretched out in the street. From behind a bullet whizzed by and struck a wall near us. We turned back from this dangerous place, and I left Der Khevont Tourian where I had found him and hurried to my house.

We worked hard, gathering our household possessions and packing our trunks and bundles, and were ready to set out. But alas, there was no one to take us away!

It was about noon. The tumult had increased. The mob spirit had begun to stir the people. Our neighbors left their houses to run to the American girls' college near by. The Turkish Army had surrounded the city. From one side the soldiers had entered the city without any resistance whatever. We too went to the American building.

Soon an American missionary, Rev. D. Gatchell, came in and said to us, "The city has been occupied by the Turks. But there is no massacre. Don't be afraid."

Thinking it my duty to go to the general who had occupied the city, Nureddin Pasha, to bid him welcome and show my respect, I proposed this undertaking to the Rev. Mr. Gatchell. He too thought it proper, and together we walked toward the American Y.M.C.A. building, which was near the quay. We would get the opinion of the Americans there about our projected visit to the pasha. They advised us to wait. In truth this advice was godsent, for just about this time, the Greek Metropolitan, with a number of Greek notables, went to Nureddin Pasha. The general received him courteously. But when the Metropolitan was returning with his men, the general ordered him arrested. There was a quick trial before the court-martial.

The death sentence was given. The Metropolitan was handed over to the Turkish mob, which carried him away. He was beaten with fists and sticks, spit at, stabbed; his beard was torn off, his eyes were gouged, his nose and ears were cut off. He died a most cruel death, one of the first victims of Smyrna.

On the way back to the American building where we had taken protection I saw a Turkish soldier driving along with his whip a young, beautiful woman, Greek or Armenian I could not tell. She was sobbing. The soldier, thinking I was an American, said, "This is a Turkish woman, and I have arrested her because she was walking unveiled."

A little farther along announcements were being distributed. I took one. It was written both in Greek and in Turkish: "Mustafa Kemal has given strict orders to the soldiers not to massacre and not to cause anyone any harm. Those who disobey will be punished with death. Let the people be assured of safety."

Stupid, credulous Armenian that I was! Totally forgetful of past experiences, I believed! Persuaded that now there was no danger, with quick, sure steps I hurried toward the girls' college to give the people there this good news. On the way I saw a Turk and a French officer going through the pockets of a Greek whom they had overpowered. Even after seeing this, still relying on the announcement, I told the people, "It is now safe enough for everyone to go back to his house." And, taking my wife and children with me, I did go back. How happy I am that without one exception all the rest did not move from their places but remained in the building! I had been the only one who believed my encouraging words!

The day was about to count its last hour. Rapes, pillaging, massacre had begun throughout the whole city. Ignorant of all this, I was waiting in my house, with my loved ones. I even went out of the house and was going to the market to buy some meat, when I heard the voice of a Turkish *çete:* "Where is your God? Let him come and save you!" Standing before the American girls' college, he was shouting to those inside.

I turned back, but still I did not think of taking my family and returning quickly to the American building. My wife had prepared lentil soup for supper. I offered the blessing and we were

193

about to eat. Suddenly there was a scream in the house next door. Our neighbors had been attacked. The *çete* were threatening them with death unless they gave them money. "We have none!" they cried.

We stood next to death. One more step and it would be our turn. My children were trembling. I was bewildered. Again the bravest among us was my wife. "To remain here is certain death," she said. "Let us open the street door and run for the American building."

I ventured to open my trunk and to take my passport and some money I had there. My wife went ahead and opened the street door. The *çete* were still busy with our neighbors. My wife told us all to take off our shoes, and running barefooted, we reached the American building safely.

As we fled from the house, I had put a red fez on my head so that if we were seen we would be taken for Turks. When we now knocked on the door, the American marine guarding it saw my fez and of course thought we were Turks and so would not let us in. My God! The American thought us Turks and locked us out! The Turk thought us Americanized and would massacre us! What were we to do?

All of us together began to cry and shout, "Please open the door quickly!"

Finally some Armenians inside heard us and recognized us and made the marine understand that we were Armenians. Then the door was opened and we fell thankfully inside.

What had been the purpose of the announcement? To instill the hope of safety in all Christians and thus to bring them out of their centers into the streets and into their houses so that the massacre could be carried on more readily. Woe unto you, accursed Turk!

It seems that I had to experience this last terrible lesson too, that I might learn well the fact that the character of the Turk was unchangeable and that deception was in his very nature. Indeed I learned this lesson, but alas, that my loved ones, because of my stupidity, were almost betrayed to death!

Darkness had finally engulfed everything. During the day many Christians had been killed; their bodies lay in the streets and in the houses. Homes and shops had been pillaged. Girls and women had been raped. The Turkish soldiers and the Turkish riffraff were now roaming unhindered throughout the whole city, doing whatever they wanted. The Armenians who were left alive crowded together in churches and other institutions, awaiting their fate. All the foreign citizens had withdrawn from the city or were about to withdraw. The consulates had been evacuated and the consuls had taken refuge in battleships. More than forty European and American battleships and transport ships were anchored before Smyrna. In the night the shots, the breaking of doors and windows, the groans of the Christians stabbed or shot and left in the streets were heard more clearly and filled us all with horror. Two thousand of us who had taken refuge in this building, crowded one on top of the other like frogs, remained completely quiet, in fear every minute of an attack.

We heard the pleadings of a small Armenian girl in the street before our building: "Mother, they are taking me away to kill me!" Her cries cut deeply into our hearts. The whole night passed in terror.

It was Sunday morning, September 10. The church bells were silent. Only in the mosques praises were rising to Allah and the Prophet was being glorified. The Armenians and the Greeks were waiting soundlessly in their hiding places so as not to betray their whereabouts to the hunters. All the noises heard in the streets, the tumult and clamor, the clatter of horses' hoofs, were the Turks'.

It was my youngest daughter's birthday. As we had celebrated the birthday of Vartan on February 11, 1920, during the massacre of Marash, so we now celebrated my daughter's birthday during the massacre of Smyrna. I pressed a kiss on her cheek and anointed my kiss with my tears. This, it seems, was to be their fortune.

I spoke to the people softly from God's living word, to give them some consolation. We prayed and offered our requests to God.

Our American benefactors, especially the president of the college, Miss Mills, were like angels, settling the people, feeding them, giving them encouragement.

Near nightfall the Gregorian church and parsonage, sheltering many Armenians, were attacked. Der Khevont Tourian, in desperation, began to ring the church bell. The mournful, melancholy toll gloomed all around, pleading for help. After an hour of horror, a company of marines was put ashore from a French battleship. They dispersed the Turks and prevented the massacre. In truth, if the European powers had wanted to, they could have helped! The marines led the Armenians to the quay, where already thousands of Christians were waiting for ships. But there they stayed.

On Monday, September 11, the situation was the same. With my own eyes I saw the Turks driving wagonloads of bombs, gunpowder, kerosene, and all else necessary to start fires. These combustibles were being arranged in and around Armenian and Greek houses and institutions as a preparation for the conflagration of the city.

Those who declare shamelessly, yea, the Turks and the French, that the Christians of Smyrna set the city on fire, let them hear the testimony of one who loves the truth. Let them know, for the sake of truth, that the city of Smyrna was set on fire purposely, by the Turks, after days of preparation.

This day it was rumored that there would be an attack on the college itself. I begged the Americans to take me and my family, under the guard of the American marines, to the battleship, since I had my passport for America, but they said it was impossible.

Another rumor had it that in a little while the Turkish officials would enter the building and take all the outstanding men out for deportation. I, my son Albert, and about ten other Armenian young men hid in the attic, a dark and dust-filled narrow place, like the stable where in 1916 I had been imprisoned. We passed a few hours here scarcely breathing. When the danger seemed over, we came down, and in great fear passed this night also.

On Tuesday, September 12, the Americans brought a number of Turkish gendarmes into the building and placed them here and there, supposedly to protect the building and those inside! Rather than easing the people, however, this terrified them even more. They would not now walk in the yard as before. No one wanted to be seen by the gendarmes. Furthermore, the gendarmes were continually going out and returning with bags on their shoulders. To arouse no suspicion in those who saw them, they would say, "We are bringing rice for you." But it was gunpowder and bombs they were bringing, and storing in secret places, to blow the place up. Whatever was being done to the other buildings in the city, the same was being done here.

Today the first steps were taken toward setting the city on fire. Flames began to soar, and one after the other, buildings turned to ashes. Many people who had hidden in them were burned alive or, rushing out, murdered.

I had seen such fires in Marash at the beginning of 1920 and was terror-stricken. With hope from all other sources gone, I went again to my everlasting fountain to drink thereof and to be satisfied. I submitted everything to God and besought him, if it were pleasing in his sight, to save us from this the seventh hell. (The other six were the massacre of 1895 in Severek, the upheaval of 1904 in Severek, the Adana massacre of 1909, the deportations of 1914-1918, the massacre of 1919 in Aleppo, and the massacre of Marash in 1920.)

It was Wednesday, September 13. The same pillaging and killing continued. My children were now exhausted and could endure this condition no longer. They were crying as well as all the other children. My heart was in anguish. My spirit was willing but my flesh was weak, and like the Man of Gethsemane, I was pleading from the depths, "Lord, if it be possible, let me not drink this cup."

At two o'clock in the afternoon all the Christian quarters of the city began to burn. Bombs exploded and wild flames roared! People rushed out into the streets like madmen and ran toward the quay. Our own section and my parsonage, with all my possessions, were in flames too. Again the bravest among us was my wife. I had handed my money and passport to Miss Mills for safekeeping. My wife went and got them. Previously we had brought a small trunk full of clothes with us. My wife directed that we all change our clothes, and leaving the old ones there, we went quickly out into the yard, ready to flee. But where? At least we were ready.

One of my best friends came to me and said, "Badveli, what's going to happen?"

I answered, "I don't know, but I feel God is about to do something!"

All two thousand men, women, and children were standing facing the large door of the building leading to the street. My family and I were now close to the door. I had one consolation, that the missionaries and the American marines would take us out of the building under the protection of their flag and lead us at least to the quay.

An American marine guarding the door called me and told me to take his place for a short time, saying he would return quickly. While we were waiting thus behind the door, suddenly someone shouted, "The building has caught fire from one side!" This clearly meant that in a little while it would explode, since bombs and gunpowder had already been placed all over it.

But even more terrible news now spread quicker than the fire: "The American missionaries and all the marines have sneaked out and fled through the small back door and we are betrayed!" I learned later that Miss Mills had refused to leave us, but the admiral had ordered the marines to take her by force.

In this crisis, the people turned to me. "What shall we do?"

"Rather than stay here and burn," I said, "open the door and let us flee toward the quay!"

The sun had sunk. But the whole city was lighted with a brighter light. We opened the door and were just about to rush out into the street when we saw the *çete* lined up before us, guns in their hands. Terrified, I drew back a step with my children to re-enter the building. But where was I going? The building was on fire! I must go forward!

I ventured forth blindly. We went on. The *çete* did not open fire on us. Perhaps they thought the Americans were coming along behind. In truth, even this illusion of America was able to prevent the Turks from massacring us!

Holding hands to keep together, my wife and children and I fled through the streets, through the flames. From every side, terror-stricken people were running toward the quay. Suddenly my son Albert espied the Americans and shouted, "The soldiers!" My wife, thinking that the Turkish soldiers were about to attack us, stopped, saying, "Leave me here and go," and dropped in a faint. My daughter Helena, seeing her mother thus, screamed, "Mother, don't die! Let me die in your stead!" Albert and I picked her up and began to drag her along with us. The children with firm steps, courageously, ran along with us. Finally, breathless, half-dead, we reached the quay.

What a hellish scene! The quay was bulging with humanity from end to end. Exhausted! Defeated! Pale! Terrified! Hopeless! The sea on one side, the flames on the other. The fire had spread so rapidly and become so intense that it devoured all before it and advanced with a roar. In a little while the magnificent buildings on the quay would also go up. And what about the people then?

The *cete* moved in and out among the people, snatching any girl who struck their eye and taking her away for rape. They drove away young men here and there too, saying they had to enlist as soldiers, but a little distance off they killed them. And those mighty battleships and brave European and American soldiers observed and took motion pictures of this hideous crime of their own contriving. Man cannot endure it! How I endured it I do not know!

We sat down on the ground so that my wife could rest for a few minutes. My son Albert wanted to go to the edge of the quay to see what was going on. This was a very dangerous undertaking, but I allowed him to go. He quickly returned with the news that the Americans were taking their citizens on board the battleship in a boat.

We immediately got up and headed there. Praise God that in this immense crowd and mix-up we did not meet any danger and were not separated. Here the American in charge was someone I knew, Mr. Jacobs by name, one of the officials of the Y.M.C.A. who, years before, when I was in office in Zeytoon, had come there. I had entertained him in my house for a number of days and taken him around to the surrounding districts. In one way or another, I had cast my bread upon the waters.

Rushing up to him I cried, "Mr. Jacobs! Save us!"

The boat being used to convey the Americans to the ship could take only four people at a time, and already there were two people in it. Mr. Jacobs allowed me to put my two smallest children in. The boat came back. This time, without waiting for permission, I threw myself into the boat and took my wife and two daughters also. Albert was left there. The boat pulled out, and I pleaded that my son be sent on the next trip. Soon we too were on the deck of the battleship *Simpson*.

But our son did not arrive. We waited two hours impatiently but still he did not come. Again, fear, doubt, woe! Perhaps he was arrested! Killed!

Two hours later, when we were transferred from the battleship to a merchant marine vessel, the *S.S. Winona*, we found our beloved son there. Now my whole family was safely on deck. We had lost everything, but, praise God, our lives had been spared.

What had happened to my son? After the boat that brought us returned, he tried to get in it but was prevented. When it had gone back and forth a few more times, he dared to throw himself into it, but the admiral of the battleship came, pulled him out, and pushed him into the crowd, saying, "Women and children first!"

Now quite hopeless, my son began to wander through the crowd. Just at this time, one of the missionaries of the college, Miss Morley, on her way to the boat, noticed him. Learning the circumstances and taking him with her, she put him on the *Winona*. In this way he was saved.

Wednesday night, September 13, I did not sleep at all. I was happy that my wife and children were resting on deck, but all night long I viewed the awful scene of Smyrna's destruction. It was now my brain that was photographing the pictures of this hell.

The quay was jammed with terror-stricken, abandoned people. The sea, as a mighty wall, stood with its silent waters to prevent escape. The roaring fire was eating its way toward the quay. The battleships of the foreign powers were anchored spectators, taking on board only their own citizens and a few others.

Turkish soldiers were robbing, abducting, raping, killing. Screams and groans, with the reaching flames, were rising toward the sky. There was no means or hope of saving the people. The battle-ships kept taking moving pictures of the conflagration. The Turk was raping and massacring the Armenian and the Greek, and the European gave his consent.

A Greek battleship wanted to bombard the Turkish quarters, but the battleships of the other powers prevented it! Before such things the human mind must burst or go mad! When the Turk kills the Christians, he must not be interfered with! When the Christian undertakes to save and protect his countrymen, he must be stopped!

Girls, pregnant women, and mothers embracing their children, rather than fall into the hands of the Turks, threw themselves into the sea and were drowned. Those men and women who knew how to swim were swimming out to the battleships. Some were taken on board but many were rejected. In fact, streams of hot water were turned on these people so they would not climb up on the ships. A man, his wife on his back, reached the ship we were on. His wife was accepted, but he was denied, and weeping he swam back to the shore.

Thousands of Armenian orphans had been let loose from their institutions. They had found their way to the quay and now were crying, pushing, sobbing, screaming!

At the time when King Constantine visited Smyrna, after the city had been taken over by the Greeks, the beautiful daughter of a well-known Greek family presented him a bouquet of flowers in the name of Smyrna. Now, at the first opportunity, this woman was caught and sent as a gift to Mustafa Kemal.

All day Thursday, September 14, the fire and the same hellish scene continued. Today the tall buildings on the quay, and also the consulates of the foreign powers, burned one after the other. Young men, Greeks and Armenians, were herded together and sent in groups to the interior, as if to be enlisted. All of them were killed. To get the earrings of women, their ears were split. To get their rings, their fingers were chopped off. And the pretty ones were always separated and taken away.

At five o'clock in the afternoon our ship, with about two thousand on board, slowly left behind and closed from our eyes

—but not from our minds—that terrible scene of Smyrna. Even in the ship there was grief. The people were hungry. They had lost everything—that too was no matter. But one was bewailing her husband. Another her parents. Still another her children. Each a loved one. Although I was happy that my family was with me, I felt deep anguish at this great loss of my countrymen.

The next afternoon we reached Greece, and soon we were in Piraeus. We rested in the building of the Greek Protestant Church.

14

From September 15 until October 12 we remained in Greece, living in a small room in an inn. New refugees came from Smyrna every day. The ships had finally begun to transport the wretched Christians.

The newcomers, filthy, scarcely human any more, brought even more horrible stories of the condition of those left behind. Few families were left intact. Most of them had been shattered and the pieces lost. This was the most tragic fact of all.

As long as I was here I tried in every way to comfort the people.

On September 25 my eyes were examined, and the doctor declared them *no bono*. This was a new worry. Nevertheless, I went to the American vice-consul, who at the same time was an able doctor. He took private care of my eyes and treated them every day.

I appealed to my benefactor, Dr. Wilson, and also to my missionary friend, Mr. Goodsell, for the expense of my journey. The former sent me five hundred dollars; the latter, three hundred.

My passport was signed again, and I bought tickets for the ship *King Alexander*. Everything was ready.

On Wednesday, September 27, I watched the Greek Army

march from Piraeus on its way to Athens. The capital city was occupied without noise or bloodshed. Constantine had fled, and his son had been declared king.

I went to Athens and visited the important places there.

On Thursday, October 12, the last examinations were performed for the ship. This time the ship's doctor declared my wife's eyes *no bono*. Would our journey be prevented? But the American vice-consul, who was there, put in a good word for me, and in the afternoon we boarded the ship. At two o'clock Friday morning, October 13, we were finally on the sea.

On October 14 we anchored before Patros. Continuing on our way, we sailed calmly on the Mediterranean. On October 20 we were on the Atlantic Ocean, and stormy and difficult sailing began. After a most anxious and dangerous journey, on October 31, Tuesday, about midnight, our ship anchored in New York harbor.

On November 1, the first- and second-class travelers were examined, and these people were taken to Ellis Island. We were third-class passengers.

On November 2 we too were transferred to Ellis Island. It seemed to me that this was America's stable. There were examinations under uncouth conditions and in embarrassing and extraordinary surroundings. My family was split up into four— my three daughters, my two sons, my wife, and I were put in different places. We had no news of one another. Perhaps deportation and massacre took place here too. The Turks used to separate families in just this way and then kill them off separately.

My children were *bono*. My eyes and my wife's eyes were doubtful. But fortunately from the first day my children found room in the quota.

For twelve days we were kept here, separated from each other. In a few days we had been informed that our children had not been murdered but were still alive! By the fourth day it appeared that my eyes were not dangerous. On the tenth day my wife was given the same assurance. Now we were together with our children.

On November 13, Monday, all of us appeared together in court. My children had been allowed to enter America. I too was permitted, as a pastor, to enter without the quota. But my wife, being born in Syria, and the Syrian quota being complete, was not accepted. I was fearful that they were going to snatch her from me. My office was to unite man and woman; these people were parting asunder what God had joined together! I wondered whether this character had been transferred to the Americans from the Turks!

Once again the Armenian came to the rescue of the Armenian. The interpreter here asked, "Is your wife educated? Has she been a teacher at any time?"

"Yes," I answered. "She has been educated in the American colleges and has taught for seven years."

"Tell that fact to the judge," he said.

I told the judge, and my wife too was accepted as a professional, without the quota.

That same day we took a train, and on Tuesday morning, November 14, we were in Buffalo, New York, in the house of my brother-in-law.

PSALM 124

IF *it had* not *been* the LORD who
was on our side, now may
Israel say;
   2 If *it had* not *been* the LORD
who was on our side, when men
rose up against us:
   3 Then they had swallowed us
up quick, when their wrath was
kindled against us:
   4 Then the waters had over-
whelmed us, the stream had
gone over our soul:
   5 Then the proud waters had
gone over our soul.
   6 Blessed *be* the LORD, who
hath not given us *as* a prey to
their teeth.

7 Our soul is escaped as a bird
out of the snare of the fowlers:
the snare is broken, and we are
escaped.

8 Our help *is* in the name of
the LORD, who made heaven and earth